P9-AEX-630

MIRROR
MIRROR

MIRROR
MIRROR
What Is My Heart Reflecting?

ALICE GRAY ♥ MARILYN McAULEY

PYRANEE
BOOKS

Zondervan Publishing House
Grand Rapids, Michigan

Mirror, Mirror

This is a Pyranee Book
Published by the Zondervan Publishing House
1415 Lake Drive, S.E., Grand Rapids, Michigan 49506

Copyright © 1986 by Alice Gray and Marilyn McAuley

Library of Congress Cataloging in Publication Data

Gray, Alice, 1939–
    Mirror, mirror.

    "Pyranee books."
    Bibliography: p.
    1. Christian life—1960–   . I. McAuley, Marilyn. II. Title.
BV4501.2.G728   1985   248.4   85-26482
ISBN 0-310-42591-X

All Scripture quotations, unless otherwise noted, are taken from THE HOLY BIBLE: NEW INTERNATIONAL VERSION (North American Edition). Copyright © 1973, 1978, 1984, by the International Bible Society. Used by permission of Zondervan Bible Publishers.

All rights reserved. No part of this publication may be reproduced, stored in a retrieval system, or transmitted in any form or by any means—electronic, mechanical, photocopy, recording, or any other—except for brief quotations in printed reviews, without the prior permission of the publisher.

Edited by Lisa Garvelink

Designed by James E. Ruark

Printed in the United States of America

To my beloved Al,
> Thank you for a love that always protects,
> always trusts, always hopes, always perseveres.

Alice

To my darling Dan,
> Precious to me are your joyful spirit and loving heart, which brilliantly reflect the beauty of Christ in your life.

Marilyn

Contents

Acknowledgments

We gratefully acknowledge our appreciation to Norman Wakefield (*Listening: A Christian's Guide to Loving Relationships*); David Augsburger (*Caring Enough to Hear and Be Heard*); and Lewis Sperry Chafer and John F. Walvoord (*Major Bible Themes*, rev. ed.). From their works we gleaned vital truths in researching chapters 7 and 8.

Opening ideas and the diagram for chapter 6 were contributed by Carol Ranstad from a lecture she presented. The introduction to chapter 7 was adapted from a lecture presented by Dee Bolen. We wish to express our grateful appreciation to these friends.

Preface

What is radiant inner beauty? Why does it spill forth with words of encouragement and acts of loving kindness? What is that gentleness revealed in the eyes and that joy bubbling from the heart? How do ears become attentive to the needs and hurts of others? How is it that some people are able to maintain a peaceful countenance during tumultuous times? What is genuine beauty? That is what *Mirror, Mirror* is all about.

Since *Mirror, Mirror* deals only with the beauty of the heart, we want to assure the reader that we also consider outward grooming an important part of the daily schedule. But as significant as that is, it's more crucial that we take time in *God's* beauty parlor for the inner self.

Concern for appearances falls into a proper perspective when our desire to look our best develops out of a deep love and reverence for our Lord. If we are children of the King of Glory, then we will want to represent Christ in a manner becoming to His name.

Spiritual grooming, however, is much more difficult than dressing and applying make-up. We must discipline ourselves daily to learn of our beautiful Lord Jesus Christ and to practice imitating Him. Ephesians 4:17−5:2 contains warnings, admonitions, and encouragement to become beautiful from the inside out.

A heart locket is lovely to look at but looking at it never seems to satisfy. We want to know what is inside. We want to see who it is the wearer holds dear to her heart. How disappointing when we open the locket and find it empty. The attractive outside loses its significance when it's empty inside.

Mirror Mirror

What is in your heart? When people converse with you, what do they discover? Is your beauty all on the surface only to be washed away at bedtime? Or have you taken the time to fill your heart with the enduring beauty of the Lord Jesus Christ? What does your heart reflect?

Come. Begin your quest for real beauty that promises eternal reward.

Part I

Changes of the Heart

So I tell you this, and insist on it in the Lord, that you must no longer live as the Gentiles do, in the futility of their thinking. They are darkened in their understanding and separated from the life of God because of the ignorance that is in them due to the hardening of their hearts. Having lost all sensitivity, they have given themselves over to sensuality so as to indulge in every kind of impurity, with a continual lust for more.

You, however, did not come to know Christ that way. Surely you heard of him and were taught in him in accordance with the truth that is in Jesus. You were taught, with regard to your former way of life, to put off your old self, which is being corrupted by its deceitful desires; to be made new in the attitude of your minds; and to put on the new self, created to be like God in true righteousness and holiness.

Ephesians 4:17–24

Mirror, Mirror

One glance at the antique mirror and I stopped abruptly. For years it had hung on the wall just inside the entry and had reflected a friendly greeting to everyone who came into our home. It was one of those decorating treasures that once found was immediately loved.

Now my heart sank. Although the beautifully crafted frame was unmarred, the mirror itself suffered a jagged crack from corner to corner. My distorted reflection in the glass reminded me of an image from a carnival house of mirrors.

A quick interrogation of my two boys produced no clues to the cause of the accident. When asked who had broken the glass, one blamed it on "I don't know," and the other on "Don't ask me"—two invisible members of our household who turn up whenever anything goes wrong.

No new evidence was discovered, and the cause of the broken mirror remained a mystery. The urgency to repair it soon gave way to the demands of a too full schedule and a too empty pocketbook. Weeks turned into months, and months into seasons. Late one spring morning, I rushed through the entry and was delighted to find a loving surprise from my husband. He had restored the mirror. What a joy to have the sparkling glass whole again. It was not until I saw my reflection that I realized how accustomed I had become to the distorted image, which had greeted me for so long. This realization left me with a nagging thought: What if all the mirrors in my life were damaged. I would soon become content with a distorted reflection.

AWARE OF CONDITIONING

The world around us promotes distortion in our lives. From almost every source, we are being conditioned to a standard of living that is marred from the one God has chosen for us as Christian women. Because we are enveloped by these wrong models, it is no wonder we begin to believe and trust in them. If we do not guard against this conditioning, we will become content with these shams.

To become more aware of the conditioning around us, I had the ladies in our neighborhood Bible study do a homework assignment. They were to look through catalogs, newspapers, and magazines to find pictures that represented what the advertising industry would have us believe to be the woman who is the fairest of them all—the woman who has everything. They were to cut these pictures out, make a collage of them, and bring their collages to Bible study the next week. What a hilarious time we had sharing our composite creations, including everything from romantic breath to hands without age spots. It didn't take long to figure out the trend. My cottage cheese cheeks and orange peel thighs were out; perfect beauty was in. I began to feel depressed.

CHILDREN ARE AFFECTED

This twisted value system of outer beauty doesn't affect adult lives only. In his book *Hide or Seek*, noted author and psychologist James Dobson points out that the obsession with beauty begins with infants.

> We adults respond very differently to an unusually beautiful child than to a particularly unattractive one and that difference has a profound impact on a developing personality. The pretty child is much more likely to see the world as warm and accepting; the ugly child is far better acquainted with the cold steel eyes of rejection.[1]

Dr. Dobson also mentions that this trend continues into the early childhood years as young children are impacted by songs like "Rudolph the Red-Nosed Reindeer" and stories like "The Ugly Duckling." The message clearly teaches that any physical abnormality makes a person unacceptable. Have you ever wondered if Sleeping Beauty would have been awakened if she had been Sleeping Ugly? Our culture provides distorted mirrors for babies as well as for adults.

MORAL STANDARDS

It's not just the emphasis on outer beauty that we need to guard against. The octopus-like media monster wraps its long tentacles around us and attempts to squeeze us into its mold of sensuality, immorality, and the occult. Recently the cable movies section of *TV Guide* caught my eye. The degeneracy of the movies' themes was discouraging: nudity, strong language, drug peddling, amphetamine addiction, alcoholism, adultery, violence, and demonism. The movies were listed alphabetically. I stopped reading at "E."

Many of today's professionals have also joined the pillage. My friend Penny sought marriage counseling because the pressures of raising three small children while her husband worked the swing shift and attended school during the day had driven her to the breaking point. The counselor's advice was explicit: "Do what will make you feel good. If this means walking out on your husband and shifting the responsibility to someone else to raise your children, do it. You have earned the right. Life is too short to spend it making someone else happy at your expense."

Marge, another married friend, went to the doctor for a routine pregnancy test at one of the largest hospitals in the area. The nurse called her a few days later with the news that the test was positive. Marge was then given her choice of two numbers to call. One was to make an appointment with an obstetrician and the other was to make an appointment for an abortion. When Marge expressed her shock and outrage at such a suggestion, the nurse merely gave a conversational shrug and explained the procedure was routine, especially when notifying someone of a second or third pregnancy. She further suggested Marge write down both numbers just in case she changed her mind.

DISCOVER GOD'S DESIGN

We have talked about the blemished values around us. God warns us of their futility and cautions us against having ignorance or hardened hearts about them. If we do not heed His warning, we will become insensitive to God's design for us and develop insatiable appetites for every kind of debasement. (Ephesians 4:17–19). While being surrounded by such a barrage of wrong representations, what does the Christian woman do? In the fourth chapter of Ephesians, God insists we behave differently than unbelievers, but how do we find the way God wants us to live? How do we rework our lives, so they are pleasing to Him?

We must exchange the mutilated concept the world has given us for the clear and perfect model of what God wants us to be. There is only one place to find the reflection we are to imitate: the Word of God. In the

Book of James, God compares His Word to a mirror. What a perfect analogy!

What is the purpose of a mirror? We look into it to see those things that need to be changed. When we are really serious about how we look, we don't choose a broken mirror, one with distortions, or one that is dirty or tinted. We want to look into the clearest mirror available. In Psalm 19, David was inspired to describe God's Word as perfect, reviving, trustworthy, right, radiant, pure, precious, and altogether righteous. What a looking glass!

TAKE ACTION NOW

God warns us about using His mirror. If we want to be blessed in all we do, we must be careful to do something about the areas of our lives that need changing. If we do not take action, we will soon forget what needs to be done (James 1:22–25).

Usually, when I look into a mirror and see something out of place, I'll fix it on the spot. But there have been those times when I am distracted or procrastinate and eventually forget all about the need until I see my reflection again. How I cringe when I realize at the shopping center that the curler or clip is still in my hair, the food still caught in my tooth, or the slip still showing. Then I wish I had taken care of it when first prompted to do so. How true God's warning is for the way we live. If we see something in His mirror that needs changing, we must take action before we forget and are pressed back into the ways of the world.

This reminds me of a Sunday School story I once read. It captured my attention and has made a lasting impact on my life.

A peddler came into a small town and parked his cart full of wares in the center of the town square. He began calling out, "Come and see my merchandise. It can change your life. It can change your life." He repeated this claim over and over. Before long, a large crowd of people had gathered in the square. It was then he uncovered his wares and revealed nothing but a cart full of mirrors. "How ridiculous," murmured the crowd and little by little, they went away shaking their heads in disgust. But three spinster ladies remained. The first one spoke up and said, "If it will change my life, I will buy a mirror."

"And so will I," said the second.

"And so will I," chimed the third.

The first one bought the smallest, fanciest mirror in the cart. On the way home she said to herself, "I do not want to look into this mirror and see myself. The mirror will have to change my life from the other room." And so she hung it in the corner of the back room, and soon the mirror was covered with dust and cobwebs.

The second spinster also bought a small, fancy mirror. On her way home she muttered, "I am much too busy doing very urgent and good things to spend my time looking into this mirror. Therefore, it will have to change my life as I glance in it occasionally." She hung the mirror in the entry and would quickly look into it from time to time as she rushed away to her busyness.

The third spinster bought a large, plain mirror. She wanted to get all the mirror she could for her money. On her way home she spoke to herself, "If I want this mirror to change my life, I must spend as much time as possible looking into it." Each morning when she awoke, she would look intently into the mirror. Before long she noticed some things that needed changing. Her dress was soiled. She washed and pressed it and even added a touch of lace. Her hair was dull and messy, so she began brushing it regularly to a beautiful shine. Even her make-up was stale and blotchy, so she scrubbed and freshened up her face. More than anything, she was pleased to discover how much better she looked when she smiled. She immediately decided to make this a prominent part of her daily dressing.

Soon people in the town began to notice the change. They stopped in to visit her and invited her over to their homes for refreshments. Before long, the most eligible widower in town began courting her, and eventually they were married.

By chance the three women who had bought the mirrors met again one day in the town square. The first two complained that although they had all bought life-changing mirrors, their lives had remained the same. The third spoke gently and explained that she had discovered the more often she looked into her mirror and did something about what she saw, the more her life had changed.[2]

CHANGES OF THE HEART

As I think back over this story, I realize I look into my mirror many times a day to check on my outward appearance. It is even more important, however, that I daily look intently into God's mirror to have my inner, spiritual life changed. God reminds us in 1 Samuel 16:7 that although we are looking at the outward appearance, God is looking at our hearts. He is looking for inner beauty at the very center of our lives, for this is the beauty that is imperishable and precious in His sight.

What place does God's mirror, the Word of God, have in your life? Are you like the first woman in the story who wanted to be changed without even looking into her mirror? Is your Bible covered with dust except on cleaning day? Or are you like the second woman who wanted to be changed with only an occasional glance? Are you so busy with good and urgent deeds that you have left out the most important work? Or finally, are you like the third woman? Do you look intently into the Scriptures and take steps to change, so your life becomes pleasing to God?

*   *   *

Mirror Mirror

Mirror, mirror on the wall, who is the fairest of them all?
The woman who turns from the ways of the world and becomes beautiful
because God's Word has changed her heart.

* * *

YOUR SPIRITUAL WORKOUT

1. What are some values in the secular world that you see shaping the attitudes and actions of our society?

2. What steps can you take to counteract these ungodly values in your own life? What about the lives of your children or the next generation as a whole?

3. Why do you think the example of a mirror is a good analogy for the Bible?

4. Total up the time you spend weekly improving your physical appearance. Include make-up, exercise, cleanliness, shopping for or making clothes, etc. Total up the time you spend weekly improving your spiritual growth. How do the two compare?

5. Think of one area of your life where you sometimes experience low self-esteem. Analyze it to determine if you are measuring yourself according to the world's standard or God's. Find one verse in Scripture to encourage you in this area. Write it out and attach it to the mirror you use most often.

NOTES

[1] James Dobson, *Hide or Seek* (Old Tappan, N.J.: Fleming H. Revell, 1974).
[2] *Mirrors,* Living Word Curriculum, Course 113 (Glendale, Calif.: Gospel Light, 1976). Used by permission.

The Purging

When you see your reflection unexpectedly in a store window, what does your appearance reveal? Are you surprised by a bright, happy countenance with eyes alive and snapping with vitality? Or do you see a rigid mouth, worry lines about the forehead, and stress around the eyes. Maybe you even exclaim to yourself, "Is this me?"

We hear how the eyes are the windows of the soul, and out of the heart the mouth speaks. We need to allow Christ to purge our worldly heart attitudes and replace them with His own. Only then will others observe an inner quality of peace and confidence that cannot be denied. We can't avoid stress, but through it, there should be a bedrock of strength in Christ. This strength will be obvious to others regardless of the circumstances we face.

Where do we place our greatest level of concentration? Is it on our marriage, family, church, friendships, or earning a living? To begin the renewing process, we must focus our greatest level of concentration on Christ.

Daily circumstances of stress and frustration need to be carefully monitored, so we don't allow them to smother the new creation within us. Personal expectations can be a great enemy to our new Christian life. When these are not met, we can fall into deep depression and become incommunicative or in a fit of anger complain endlessly. We expect our family to fit certain molds; if they don't, we add another rock to our pile of stress. We expect the minister to preach a certain way; if he doesn't, we either move to another church or stay and cause discord. We expect friends to respond positively to our peculiarities; if they don't, we develop sharp edges. Finally, there are the expectations we place on ourselves, becoming our own worst enemies if we can't meet or even exceed them. There is only one person who can be everything to everyone: our Lord.

SELFISH EXPECTATIONS

One Christmas I was giving a formal dinner for some friends. I had focused on perfection—perfection for my home, my meal, and myself. The artistic attraction of my gourmet dinner was a multicolored, layered gelatin salad in a large, crown mold. I had spent considerable time that day constructing it, all the while imaging how stunning it would look, and the raves it would inspire.

I was about to turn the gelatin onto the sterling silver platter when the doorbell rang. The guests had arrived early. Quickly I turned the mold over and felt the soft plop on the tray. When the mold was removed, to my horror, the crown of the salad was still in the mold and the mess on the plate looked like a miniature Grand Canyon! Failure to meet my expectations plummeted my spirit into the depths of despair.

I wish I could say my guests had been my primary concern, but just then I felt there was nothing on earth as important as the ridiculous blob of gelatin wobbling before me. Everything was picture perfect except the gelatin and my attitude!

The Purging

This is a homey example and certainly not one of very great consequence, but it seems to be the little, seemingly insignificant things that expose our inner life. If I had reflected on the needs of others instead of on perfection, I would have saved myself a great deal of stress and disappointment. Unfulfilled expectations can be devastating.

It's sad when we lose control, but if the situation can be used as a stepping stone in our growth, then it has a seed of merit. Many times since then, I've had similar failures but I very clearly remember the wobbly gelatin. By God's strengthening grace, I've been able to put these situations into proper perspective.

Though a Christian, I had not put off all the old attitudes spoken of in Ephesians 4:23–24. I was something like my gelatin. I was being made new but still holding on to old attitudes. I needed remolding into God's image.

Allowing God to remold our minds will enable us to display consistently the new disposition He is creating in us—a disposition that is holy and righteous. Righteousness is possible. It's more than a big word used by theologians. It's the character of Christ manifested in our daily lives. As we learn the truth that is in Him, our minds will be renewed. They will no longer be conformed to the pattern of the world. Instead we will desire to live holy lives and will be able to know God's will for us (Romans 12:2). We will also benefit from the rewards of living righteously. What are those rewards? Isaiah 32:17 tells us "The fruit of righteousness will be peace; the effect of righteousness will be quietness and confidence forever."

ASSESSING OURSELVES

Since we do not belong to the world but to Christ, it is necessary to keep a constant check on our lives. Regular assessment is a healthy process for a Christian. Let's take a moment now to do some assessing. Ask yourself:

Mirror Mirror

1. What are the priorities in my life?

2. Whom do I try to please—God or people?

3. Am I practicing the principles of God's word or the principles of the world?

4. Is my life characterized by peace and confidence?

These probing questions penetrate through the crustiness of our soul into the tender, sensitive areas of our spirit—our inner dwelling—that place where Christ, in His Spirit, is living and working. It is His art studio where He is remolding us from our former way of life into His image—an image of love, joy, peace, patience, kindness, goodness, faithfulness, gentleness, and self-control (Galatians 5:22–23). He invites us to come in and observe Him at work. He wants us to focus on Him and cooperate with Him.

Review your answers to the above questions and determine how they affect your response to the troublesome issues of life. If your spouse walked in from work tonight and announced the loss of a job, what would your first reaction be? How would you handle the news of your unmarried son saying he had gotten a girl pregnant or your daughter saying she had to get married?

Is your initial thought "What will others think?" or "I'll never be able to face the people at church"? Or do you think first of the agony your loved one is experiencing and the injury done to Christ's reputation? Your *initial* reaction will indicate on whom you focus the most and whom you really love—yourself or God and others?

Reading the memoirs of Rose Kennedy, I was deeply impressed with an incident involving one of her sons. He wrecked the family car, and when his father heard the news, his first words were, "Was he hurt?" rather than, "How ruined is the car?" Those words came back very vividly the day my own son drove in with a crumpled bumper on my car. Did my concern center on my car or my son? How quickly I could have injured my son emotionally had I given the impression I loved my car more than him.

BITTER OR BETTER?

We've observed situations from mundane, daily annoyances to some of the deeper issues in life. How we respond to these events reveals much about our real selves and our devotion to Christ.

All of us will experience problems of one degree or another. They can make us bitter or they can make us better. Because of our free will, it's up to us how we handle situations, but God desires to use suffering as a time for us to grow and become stronger in our faith and love for Him.

C. H. Spurgeon wrote, "We need affliction as the trees need winter, that we may collect sap and nourishment for future blossoms and fruit. Sorrow is as necessary for the soul as medicine is to the body." Let your times of suffering count for eternity.

We need to continually reassess our walk with God and determine if we are allowing our spirit to be malleable as Christ remolds us in His image. Once we let down our guard, how quickly our inner dwelling gets cluttered and how painful cleaning it up can be. But if we focus on losing our lives for Christ's sake, He will sustain us as He performs the necessary changes. The Holy Spirit will give us the power and strength to endure the purging. God's grace will be sufficient when we need it—not *before,* but *when* we need it. The reward is finding our lives pleasing to God. Suddenly there is a depth of meaning to life that we never experienced before. We *can* become better. God gives us the choice.

BEWARE OF THE MATERIAL WORLD

So many times our responses to unexpected problems show us how corrupt our desires are. We realize how caught up in the material world we have become. From the time we are born, we are developing our senses of taste, touch, sight, sound, and smell. Everything around us seems tangible. The major section of our learning life revolves around concrete experiences. Many people refuse to acknowledge any belief that they can't measure or observe. But in truth, we are very much a part of the spirit world. God is spirit, and we worship Him in spirit.

God gives us guardian angels for protection, and the angels rejoice over each soul that accepts Christ. These two truths reveal the angels' awareness of us. Though they, being spirit, are essentially different from our physical form, they are an important part of life on earth.

Satan and the demon world also observe us, and we certainly are aware of the temptation they inflict on us. We are warned in Scripture that "our struggle is not against flesh and blood, but against the powers of this dark world and against the spiritual forces of evil in the heavenly realms" (Ephesians 6:12).

Greatest of all wonders is the promise that God Himself, in the form of the Holy Spirit, has chosen to dwell within the bodies of believers. The moment we receive Christ as Savior and commit our lives to Him, the Holy Spirit indwells us and promises never to leave us. His spirit within us is greater than all of Satan's power outside us.

Since we are made up of spirits and bodies, balance between our physical and spiritual life is as necessary as it is between flood and drought in nature. Keeping that balance gives us a clearer perspective of what is most important. Giving Christ first place in our lives puts everything else in its proper order.

The Purging

CHANGE FROM WITHIN

Once our perspective is right, we come to the point where change begins in our spirit, in the center of what is real. All too often we have become clever at covering up our real selves and showing to others an imitation of holiness and righteousness that is strictly external. No matter how skilled we become at this charade, there will come those times when we are caught unaware and the overflow of our heart is seen for what it really is.

Christ wants to purge our inner being so we no longer have to continue the masquerade. He wants our outer actions of righteousness and holiness to be a true manifestation of our inner being.

In the story of *The Velveteen Rabbit,*[1] there's an encounter in the nursery between two of the toys. The newcomer is Velveteen Rabbit and he is asking the wise old Skin Horse what it means to be Real. Skin Horse tells him it isn't how you are made but a thing that happens to you.

The rabbit then asks if it hurts to become Real. The horse answers, "Sometimes . . . when you are Real you don't mind being hurt."

The rabbit wonders if it happens all at once or bit by bit. The Skin Horse says, "It doesn't happen all at once. You become. It takes a long time. That's why it doesn't often happen to people who break easily, or have sharp edges, or who have to be carefully kept. Generally, by the time you are Real, most of your hair has been loved off, and your eyes drop out and you get loose in the joints and very shabby. But these things don't matter at all, because once you are Real you can't be ugly, except to people who don't understand."

The rabbit asked the horse if he were Real. Skin Horse smiled and replied, ". . . once you are Real you can't become unreal again. It lasts for always."

Finally the Velveteen Rabbit sighed. He wanted to be Real, but wondered if he could handle the discomfort involved.

WILL THE REAL YOU PLEASE STAND UP

Do you want to become real? Are you tired of pretending to be what you are not? Do you want to change even if the process is uncomfortable?

We have briefly covered some complex spiritual truths that will be dealt with more completely in the succeeding chapters. Take time to read thoughtfully and ask our Lord to help you smooth out the rough places. Accept His loving invitation to work with Him in the studio of your heart.

We begin by coming to Christ and knowing Him. We respond as He gently beckons us with these words, "Come to me . . . and learn from me. . . ." (Matthew 11:28–29).

To learn from Him, we study His ways, His truth, His life. The wise apostle Paul writes in Philippians 3:8, "I consider everything a loss compared to the surpassing greatness of knowing Christ Jesus my Lord."

To know Christ we must:

1. Assess our priorities and put Him first.

2. Evaluate whom we are trying to please and then determine to please God.

3. We must analyze the principles we practice and change those that do not agree with God's principles.

4. We must measure our ability to live a life of peace by placing our confidence in Christ.

As we begin to know Christ, we will see ourselves in a new way. We will see attitudes and desires that are marred, corrupt, and ugly. We must cast them away and replace them with the new likeness of God.

Does it happen all at once? No, it doesn't. We become. And what we become is very real.

The Purging

* * *

What we give God, he takes;
What God takes, he cleanses;
What he cleanses, he fills;
What he fills, he uses.

* * *

YOUR SPIRITUAL WORKOUT

1. Review your answers to the four questions under the section "Assessing Ourselves" on pages 23 and 24, and the four conditions for knowing Christ on page 28. How do they compare? What changes do you need to make?

2. Examine your attitude toward materialism. Which of your possessions would you be most distressed about losing? List them on a sheet of paper and offer them up to God to use for his honor and glory. Remove yourself from your ownership of them and thank God for letting you take care of them for Him.

3. What are some of your personal expectations of yourself and your family?

4. What are some expectations others have about you?

5. How do these expectations cause you stress and how can you bring them into balance?

6. For encouragement, memorize Isaiah 32:17,

   The fruit of righteousness will be peace;
   the effect of righteousness will be
   quietness and confidence forever.

NOTES

[1] Margery Williams, *The Velveteen Rabbit*, (New York: Doubleday, 1958), 17, 20.

Part II
Decisions of the Heart

Therefore each of you must put off falsehood and speak truthfully to his neighbor, for we are all members of one body. "In your anger do not sin": Do not let the sun go down while you are still angry, and do not give the devil a foothold. He who has been stealing must steal no longer, but must work, doing something useful with his own hands, that he may have something to share with those in need.

Do not let any unwholesome talk come out of your mouths, but only what is helpful for building others up according to their needs, that it may benefit those who listen. And do not grieve the Holy Spirit of God, with whom you were sealed for the day of redemption. Get rid of all bitterness, rage and anger, brawling and slander, along with every form of malice. Be kind and compassionate to one another, forgiving each other, just as in Christ God forgave you.

Ephesians 4:25–32

Truth for a Change

Faded blue jeans, old tennis shoes, and drab T-shirts dominated the scene. As though determined not to blend in with the crowd, one spunky little grandma wore a florescent pink sweatshirt decorated with bold purple letters. They loudly announced that she was an "oldie but goodie." I chuckled at her originality and noticed others who had also chosen unique outfits. Though some people were innovative, all were appropriately dressed for camping.

I set my imagination free to consider how different this same group of people would look donned in garb suitable for job interviews, weddings, snow skiing, or graduation. It tickled my thoughts to wonder what delightful creation the perky grandmother would wear to an aerobics class.

OUR SPIRITUAL WARDROBE

To be appropriately dressed for various activities, it is obvious we need changes in our wardrobe. This same simple principle is also true in the spiritual realm. Ephesians 4:17−32 teaches us to cast off all things that are not suitable for our walk with Christ. In their place, we are to put on what is designed to identify us with righteousness and holiness. How are you dressed today?

PUT OFF FALSEHOOD—PUT ON TRUTHFULNESS

The need for truth is so essential that the apostle Paul lists it first among seven wardrobe changes. Most of us do not readily admit we have a problem with veracity. Instead we try to camouflage it with all sorts of excuses: "It's only a *white* lie; a little exaggeration never hurt anyone; the end justifies the means; everybody does it."

Just this week I was explaining to a dear Christian friend about my own personal struggles with total truthfulness. I was sharing some of the ways I am tempted to justify this problem in my life. Although she is sincere in her growing walk with the Lord, she candidly stated, "Oh, I don't have any problem with lying. I just distort the truth."

No wonder we have trouble casting it aside. We disguise it so well, we don't even realize we are wearing falsehood.

Webster defines a lie as a "falsehood with an intention to deceive." St. Augustine's definition is "having one thing in one's heart and uttering another with the intent to deceive." Truthfulness would obviously be the antidote to lying.

On the surface, it would appear to be an easy decision to wear truthfulness habitually. In practice, the moral issue becomes complicated. Must we be ruthlessly honest to the sick and dying? Are there not social graces where white lies are the best choice? Is telling all that we know necessary for truth? Are there not times when the consequences of truth are worse than deceitfulness?

In this chapter, we will address these issues briefly. As we do so, however, God's standard not man's will be the gatekeeper of our conclusions.

IN THE BEGINNING

It was Adam and Eve who were first betrayed by a lie. Satan's distortion of truth about God certainly fits Webster's definition. His intention was to deceive. Satan was successful with Eve, and throughout history, his tactics have not changed. He is identified in the New Testament as the Deceiver and Father of Lies.

Beginning with Genesis where the first lie was uttered and ending with Revelation 22:15 where people who love and practice falsehoods are listed among those who will not be in heaven, God's displeasure with lying does not change.

It is prohibited in the ninth commandment. It is listed as one of the seven things God hates in Proverbs 6. Jesus addresses truthfulness in the Sermon on the Mount. It is here Christ teaches that our yes should mean yes and our no should mean no without the necessity of taking an oath.

William Barclay's commentary on this and on the companion passage in James 5:12 gives added insight:

> The great Greeks held that the best guarantee of any statement was not an oath but the character of the man who made it; and that the ideal was to make ourselves such that no one would ever think of demanding an oath from us because he would be certain that we would always speak the truth.
>
> The New Testament view is that every word is spoken in the presence of God and ought, therefore, to be true; and it would agree that the Christian must be known to be a man of such honor that it will be quite unnecessary ever to put him on oath. The New Testament would not entirely condemn oaths but it would deplore the human tendency to falsehood, which on occasion makes oaths necessary.[1]

I have mentioned but a few of the numerous passages throughout Scripture that clarify God's immutable position on lying. He abhors it because He is the absolute Truth.

STARK CONTRAST

Unlike God's immutability, the world's moral standard is rapidly declining. Daniel Yankelovich, contributing editor of *Psychology Today*, points out that advertising techniques in the past have been a good mirror of changing norms in our society. Recent changes in advertising are clues that the social norms about lying are growing weaker. "We are accustomed to ads that make extravagant claims, but ads that make a joke of lying, conveying the message that it's okay to bend the truth to get what you want, are something new."[2]

Although some forms of deception in everyday private life have always been present, Yankelovich is quick to point out that new forms of public lying are beginning to surface in the common areas where we do the business of society. He states that they represent a threat to the standards of truth that regulate our behavior toward each other.

As we see acceptability and frequency of lying permeate our culture, we must begin to ask about the consequences. In her noteworthy book *Lying: Moral Choice in Public and Private Life*, Sissela Bok ponders deception in society. "Imagine a society, no matter how ideal in other respects, where word and gestures could never be counted upon. Questions asked, answers given, information exchanged—all would be worthless."[3]

We normally think of society as a large, organized structure of people where we have little impact. But as we ask questions about the consequences of dishonesty in society, we must ask these same questions about relationships with our friends, our families, our fellow employees, and our neighbors. In asking these questions, we should determine our responsibility to truthfulness.

WHY DO WE LIE?

The reasons for lying are as diverse as the ways we do it. We lie to get what we want, to hurt, to protect, to avoid certain embarrassing consequences, to gain personal profit, or perhaps to have something as simple as a legitimate-sounding excuse. The same decadence that has affected the rest of our moral standards has rotted our integrity. Lying is often accepted and even encouraged.

Pat Collins, Arts and Entertainment Editor for CBS, endorses lying in some situations. In her book *How To Be A Really Nice Person*, she says of total honesty:

> It's self-indulgent, destructive, hurtful, even cruel, and not at all nice.
> It is more than time to restore the white lie to its rightful and extremely important place in human affairs.[4]

Although Ms. Collins' viewpoint is based primarily on a need for social grace, God's standard disagrees with her logic.

How grateful I am for the balance and inspiration that Nobel prize winnner Alexandr Solzhenitsyn brings to this subject with these inspirational words: "Simple is the ordinary courageous human being's act of not participating in the lie, of not supporting false actions! What his stand says is: 'So be it that *this* takes place in the world, that it even reigns in the world—but let it not be with my complicity.' "[5]

HOW DO WE LEARN TO LIE?

The encroachment on integrity surrounds us. Early in life, children learn that dishonesty seems to pay. They do not realize its pleasure is only for a season, and the young begin to lie for all the same reasons adults do.

Mirror Mirror

Disregard for truth invades our homes in a variety of ways. Children watch many hours of television, and studies continue to prove this element to be an aggressive value conditioner. We must be faithful in our vigil to teach our children to be selective in their viewing and to evaluate the principles condoned on many programs.

Music also plays a strong role in shaping moral choices of our young people. Space does not permit my delving into this whole area. I only plead that you be aware of the words to which your children are listening. Help them to discern the philosophy that repetitiously undermines the teaching of God's Word. It is wise to listen to our own music choices with the same questions in mind.

As the powerful arm of humanistic teaching strengthens its grip, the educational system becomes another partner in shaping values of truthfulness. Occasional classes and infrequent examples of values clarification are no longer the main enemy. A false gradation of moral choices has permeated the entire system and has become so homogenized into the apparatus of education, that it is now impossible to isolate. Children are taught to accept what appears to be good rather than to think through and then choose the highest value.

WHOOPS! OUR OWN STANDARDS ARE SHOWING

Before we place too much blame on other factors, we must stop and scrutinize ourselves.

The story is told of the embarrassed mother whose son had been helping a friend fix up a secondhand car. When the friend sold the car, the son bragged to his mom that he had helped get a good price. "I showed Dave that same trick Dad used to turn back the mileage when we sold our old car."

What is our reaction to Pat Collins' encouragement to involve everyone in the household so that a white lie can be successful? She specifically advises that every child old enough to answer the phone should be involved. Her advice is to make certain they are aware of each detail of the lie to help with the cover-up if necessary.[6]

If we are offended at her suggestion, then we must be ruthlessly honest about any double standards we have. Our children learn by example. Do they hear idle threats, broken promises, gossip, exaggeration, careless or intentional lies? If they see us engaged in untruthfulness, they will assume this is our standard. We must realize we are significant role models. Even what we do in moderation, our children use as an excuse to do in excess.

We state we are committed to truthfulness. Do our actions prove that commitment? Or are we giving hand-me-downs to the next generation that indicate lying is acceptable attire?

HOPE FOR A CHANGE

Do you feel helpless in the battle for truth? Does it seem too late? Is the challenge too hard or the picture too bleak? Take courage. There is hope. It is in the darkest place that a single candle has its greatest impact.

I am reminded of the time our family was on a tour of the Oregon Caves. We had ventured far inside the cavern and wound in and around many passages before our tour guide came to an abrupt stop. In the deepest part of the cave, he explained that all the lights along the path as well as those positioned overhead would be turned out for a moment. He carefully explained we should remain calm because he was equipped with a powerful flashlight in case there were any mishaps bringing the lights back on.

It was a dreadful moment when the absolute blackness engulfed us. Fear gripped me as I choked back nausea and felt perspiration leap from every pore. Then there was relief when a single match was lit . . . then another and another. The need for light seemed to be as contagious as the joy it brought. Soon the pathway and overhead lights were relit, and fear retreated.

Our world is a dark place, but even a single light brings comfort. As we commit ourselves to truthfulness, our friends, family, and business associates will sense relief and joy. Truth can be wonderfully contagious.

THE WHOLE TRUTH AND NOTHING BUT THE TRUTH?

In these brief pages, we have attempted to illuminate the need for Christians to speak nothing but the truth. Speaking the *whole* truth is another aspect we must consider. At this juncture, we will again remember it is God's Word that will be the gatekeeper for our conclusions.

There will be times when telling all we know will be harmful; times when someone will not be able to bear all the truth. It is then we will be tempted once again to put on the garment of falsehood. We must not. Instead, let us carefully choose the timing of our words, how much to say, and how it should be said. Remember, truth is only part of the wardrobe. We must also wear love, patience, kindness, and gentleness.

God Himself has not revealed all He knows to us.[7] Jesus Christ did not answer wholly and directly every question asked. Many times He remained silent or replied with a parable or a question. And yet His silence or His answer was never deceptive.

Scripture teaches we must speak the truth *in love*. We must also speak only those things that are helpful for building others up according to their needs. These principles must be our guideline before we speak the whole truth.

Truth for a Change

THE FINAL LIFELINE FOR TRUTH

There is one more struggle. On occasions it will appear as though the greatest good will result from a lie rather than from truth. These situations will cause us to wrestle with logic and rationalization until they engulf us in a sea of confusion. It is then we will need a lifeline for truth. That lifeline is obedience and trust in God.

We must know this lifeline is so secure that we can depend on it rather than on our own reasoning. With total confidence, we must be willing to place ourselves and our circumstances in the hands of our powerful, sovereign, loving God who does not need the help of lying to accomplish His purposes.

We need to trust Him even when truth seems to mean failure. God has already taught us that what sometimes appears to be defeat is actually victory. Consider the Cross. Then look beyond it to the triumphant Resurrection. When we acknowledge all that the Resurrection means, we begin to understand that God can and will accomplish everything He has promised to do. In His time, righteousness will be victorious!

Knowing this victory is one of the truths that set us free.

* * *

It is always easier to study and comprehend truth than it is to be truth.[8]

* * *

YOUR SPIRITUAL WORKOUT

1. Think of several situations where you might consider a white lie as your only option. Examine several honest alternatives for each situation and choose the best.

2. Think back to your childhood and list some ways your values about truthfulness were formed. Compare them with the principles mentioned on telling the whole truth in this chapter.

3. If asked whether you value truthfulness, how would you respond? How do your actions prove your answer? Where is there a need for change in your life?

4. Study Proverbs 6:16–19. Write a statement about what you learned about lying.

5. Review a recent conversation with a close friend. What did it reveal about your standard of truthfulness?

6. Write a prayer of commitment from your heart to God telling Him of your sorrow for past lies, your new commitment to truth, and praise for His promise to strengthen you.

NOTES

[1] William Barclay, *The Letters of James and Peter,* The Daily Study Bible (Philadelphia: Westminster, 1976).
[2] "Lying Well Is The Best Revenge," *Psychology Today* (August 1982).
[3] Sissela Bok, *Lying: Moral Choice in Public and Private Life* (New York: Pantheon, 1978). The author teaches ethics and decision making in medicine at Harvard Medical School and is a member of the Ethics Advisory Board of the U.S. Secretary of Health, Education and Welfare.
[4] Pat Collins with John Malone, *How to Be a Really Nice Person: Doing the Right Thing Your Way* (New York: M. Evans and Co., 1983).
[5] Alexandr I. Solzhenitsyn, *The Nobel Lecture on Literature* (New York: Harper & Row, 1972).
[6] Collins with Malone, *How to Be a Really Nice Person.*
[7] First Corinthians 13:9; Deuteronomy 29:29; Isaiah 55:8–9.
[8] Joseph C. Aldrich, *Life-Style Evangelism* (Portland, Oreg.: Multnomah, 1981).

CHAPTER **4** BY MARILYN

Heaven's Signal

As my husband and I received friends at our wedding reception, a dear elderly man who was a spiritual giant in our church handed his gift to us. He hadn't bothered to wrap it because he wanted to share a pearl of wisdom with us right away. His gift was a book, and his pearl was the following inscription: "Do not let the sun go down while you are still angry" (Ephesians 4:26). It made a profound impact on both of us. We've never forgotten that pearl of wisdom. Perhaps that's one of the reasons our marriage has been a happy one.

One delightful, gray-haired couple in our church also takes God's warning seriously. They will not go to bed if differences have not been resolved. They drolly share how on occasions they have spent whole nights sitting up waiting for resolutions.

God provides a colorful reminder every evening in sunsets. They are His final revelry of the day and announce the coming of night. Sunsets are His signal to make peace. Night is coming but rest won't, if peace is not prevailing.

WHAT IS ANGER?

Anger is described by many adjectives. Frustrated, discouraged, peeved, irritated, anxious, fearful, hurt, worried, depressed, annoyed, put-out, uptight, humiliated, and grieved are but a few describers.

Anger is an emotion created by God. God expects us to use that emotion wisely and gives us principles to help us control anger.

According to Ephesians 4:26–27, the phrase "in your anger" assumes that anger is a viable emotion. The command following those words, "do not sin," is to be carefully obeyed. We are to keep close accounts so we don't "let the sun go down" while we are still angry. This means there's no time to nurse a grudge or be unforgiving. Finally, we are not to give Satan the opportunity to conform us to his image—"do not give the devil a foothold" (Ephesians 4:27).

Chuck Swindoll created a good working definition of anger in his book *Three Steps Forward Two Steps Back:* "Anger is an emotional reaction of hostility that brings personal displeasure, either to ourselves or to someone else."[1]

Dr. Richard Dobbins says of anger,

> In its simplest form, anger is unexpressed energy.
>
> Physiologically, this is exactly what it is. When your mind interprets some situation as threatening, a biochemical reaction is triggered which results in the creation of unusually large amounts of energy for your use in facing the perceived threat. Your emotion of anger is thus transformed into physical energy.
>
> Until you determine what form the expression of your energy will take, you have committed no sin. Your moral challenge is this: you are responsible to determine what you will do with the energy your anger has created.
>
> If a person can't admit he is angry, he will have great difficulty learning healthy ways of discharging the energy his anger has created. Therefore . . . accept anger as a fact of your life. Realize that you are

entitled to experience anger without guilt or shame so long as you learn to express it appropriately.[2]

The authors of *Anger is Choice* say, ". . . Anger in itself is neither good nor bad. It is just anger. It is an emotion. . . . The problem with anger is the direction in which it leads you. Or better stated, which direction you allow your anger to go."[3]

David Augsburger, in *Caring Enough to Confront,* defines anger as "A demand that also demands others meet your demands. . . . Even though you seldom put the demands into words, they are there inside the feelings, energizing the resentment."[4]

God has provided us with anger for protection against harm and injustice. More often we use it for retaliation to hurt someone who has, knowingly or unknowingly, hurt us. Unspoken expectations and selfish demands are flints that spark emotion into the wrong use of anger.

HOW DO YOU HANDLE YOUR ANGER?

How does anger affect your life—physically, emotionally, mentally, and spiritually?

The various degrees of anger have been described as beginning with mild irritation and progressing through the stages of indignation, wrath, fury, and finally, the most dangerous form of anger: rage.

Psychiatrist David Viscott outlines the relationship of anger to other feelings in an interesting cycle, placing anger in perspective with anxiety, hurt, guilt, and depression. The cycle he describes begins with anxiety, which is the expectation of *future hurt or loss.* When such a loss occurs, he describes the next feeling as hurt or *present pain* that gives a sense of sadness or depletion. The response to hurt moves into anger that is *past pain expressed* to those around you. It is the feeling of wanting to hurt someone. Another response to hurt can be guilt that is *past pain unexpressed.* This is, in reality, anger held in and turned against yourself. Guilt, from this *chronically unexpressed anger* can develop into depression. This pattern of reacting to hurt by holding in anger depletes your energy and makes you feel lifeless.[5]

After speaking about prayer at a junior high girls' retreat, I asked the girls to share how God had helped them through a trial. Some answers to prayer were related, and then one of the leaders we'll call Linda, a quiet, sensitive woman in her thirties, told us how she became a widow.

She and her husband had been married three years and were the proud parents of one small child. One day at work a young man in a wild rage shot Linda's husband. The young man did not even know the man he had murdered. But his uncontrolled rage left a man dead, a young woman widowed, and a toddler fatherless. Even though the murderer was sent to prison, Linda continued to struggle with grief and anger. She wondered what it would take to move her beyond these relentless emotions. In this one episode, we see two types of anger: quick, explosive anger and repressed anger.

Those who have a short fuse explode volcanically. They are frightening to be near when words of abuse pour forth, objects fly, and in extreme cases, lives are in danger. When their rage is spent, they walk away feeling better but leave in their wake injured egos, crushed emotions, and devastated souls. Quick rage indicates low self-control. A study by M. K. Biaggio, professor of psychology at the University of Idaho, found that students quick to express anger were less healthy than those who restrained themselves.[6]

On the other hand, repressed or denied anger creates a host of problems, too. Many people deny their anger while a long, slow fuse is burning within them. This is what Linda experienced.

The denial of anger is particularly prominent among Christians, since they have been taught to believe anger is not an acceptable emotion. This is a dangerous attitude that has an adverse effect on the world, the church, the family, and the person.

In *Healing for Damaged Emotions,* Dr. David Seamands lists six symptoms in identifying the perfectionist complex. The last two are anger and denial. He says, "Too often the anger is not faced but denied. Because anger is considered a terrible sin, it is pushed down. And the whole mixture of bad theology, legalism, and salvation by performance becomes a frozen Niagara. This is when deep emotional problems set in. Mood changes are so great and so terrible, such a person seems to be two different people at the same time."[7]

Dr. Henry Brandt, a leading Christian psychologist, says anger is involved in 80 to 90 percent of all counseling.[8] So far we have seen that both volatile and subtle anger is to be considered equally serious. Physically, emotionally, mentally, and spiritually, wrong anger can cause great suffering.

HOW'S YOUR PHYSICAL HEALTH?

Dr. Seamands wrote, "Satan knows your weaknesses; he understands your infirmities and uses them to great advantage against you. . . . He knows how to exploit your weaknesses in the direction of discouragement, disappointment, failure, and abdication of the Christian life. . . . Some of the most powerful weapons in Satan's arsenal are psychological. Fear is one of these. Doubt is another. Anger, hostility, worry, and of course, guilt. Long-standing guilt is hard to shake off; it seems to hang on even after a Christian claims forgiveness and accepts pardoning grace."[9]

Our emotional center is in the brain. All our nerve fibers go out from that point to every organ in the body. No wonder what we think is expressed in how we feel, act, and look.

What is your particular ailment? Have you pushed resentments, hurts, and anxieties so far down, you've forgotten about them? You may have allowed your conscious mind to forget them, but your subconscious gnaws away until finally your body relents. Many physical ailments are rooted in anger. Medical researchers have discovered that bitter emotions can actually prevent healing. When physical ailments are the result of emotional stress, they are considered psychosomatic disorders.

Psychosomatic illness is a very real physical condition. It's brought on by the body's reaction to stress. Our reaction to stress is more to blame than the stress itself. We throw pity parties, nurse grudges, cherish pet peeves, stew and worry something to death, and then wonder why we're sick and depressed.

It's well-known that ulcers, high blood pressure, heart trouble, respiratory and digestive problems, skin ailments, nervous disorders, obesity, anorexia nervosa, bulimia, arthritis, and a host of other ailments are often attributable to some degree of anger. Anger demands a high price. Chuck Swindoll was right when he said, "Anger is no humorous matter. Unless understood, admitted and kept under control it will slay us."[10] Anger seeks release and will find it one way or another.

HOW'S YOUR SPIRITUAL HEALTH?

Negative anger injures our spiritual life, too. Isaiah 59:2 says, "But your iniquities have separated you from your God; your sins have hidden his face from you, so that he will not hear." With sin in our lives, we are like colicky babies. We're constantly crying to God and wondering why we're not getting results. Confession opens the channel of communication with God.

Psalm 38 is David's petition telling God the agony he feels over sin in his life. He pleads with God not to rebuke him in His anger or discipline him in His wrath. Then he proceeds to explain all that is wrong with him.

He recognizes his sin has created great physical, mental, emotional, and spiritual discomfort in his life. Proverbs 21:2 says, "All a man's ways seem right to him, but the Lord weighs the heart."

David's heart weighed heavy with sin. But the weight of the heart can be made lighter by confession of sin. David confessed his sin and so can you. Ask Christ to change you from within so you may reflect his radiance through a genuinely happy and healthy body, mind, and spirit.

THE POWER OF ATTITUDE

As we witness the ravages of the Holocaust through the various media presentations, we grieve over the atrocities that were committed. To think anger was at the root of the problem makes us aware of how violent this emotion can be.

Knowing what you do about concentration camps and prisons, have you considered how you would handle yourself if you were in captivity and under the domination of another power?

Dr. Viktor Frankl, a survivor of Nazi concentration camps, said, "We who lived in concentration camps can remember the men who walked through the huts comforting others, giving away their last piece of bread. They may have been few in number, but they offer sufficient proof that everything can be taken from a man but one thing: the last of the human freedoms—to *choose one's attitude* in any given set of circumstances, to choose one's way" (italics mine).[11]

In an interview, Polish Solidarity leader Lech Walesa was asked, "Are you not something of a double hostage—both of the authorities who guard you and the church that protects you?" He answered, "I am always free, even when I am in prison! My thoughts, my dreams, my aspirations cannot be physically destroyed. The truth is always the truth."[12]

Linda, the young widow, finally made peace with herself and with God by going to the prison and forgiving her husband's murderer. She left that prison unshackled from the chains of unforgiveness. She was able to walk away with a light heart.

The apostle Paul was often in chains but only in the flesh. His spirit was free. He ministered to the guards who were chained to him. In prison he wrote the Epistles that give us so much encouragement today. The saints came to him while he was in chains and *he* encouraged them.

These people are telling us from experience that we do have a choice in the decision of our attitudes. We do not have to be prisoners in our spirit. We can command our will to obey God even in captivity, and our spirit will soar beyond the walls that confine us. We always have the freedom to choose how we will behave.

CONTROLLING ANGER

Paul tells us in Ephesians 5:15–21 how to control anger. First, he admonishes us to be wise and careful and to purchase every opportunity that comes our way to minister for Christ. Then he wants us to understand what the Lord's will is for us. We are to be filled with the Holy Spirit. If we are filled with the Holy Spirit, there will be a song on our lips; music that honors Christ quenches destructive anger. With a song in the heart, we will be thankful people; a happy heart is a grateful heart. Finally, we are to submit to one another out of reverence for Christ; a servant's heart cannot cohabit with a grudging heart . . . the anger will have to leave.

If angry grudges are keeping you from having a song in your heart, you need to confront the issue and get the air cleared. But remember to attack the problem and not the person. Carefully pray and plan before you discuss the offense with the offender, remembering you are capable of committing the same offense. Galatians 6:1 warns us, "But watch yourself, or you also may be tempted."

By understanding anger, knowing God's will, and employing a right attitude, we have a better opportunity not to be caught off guard the next time the emotion of anger rises.

THE KEY TO FREEDOM

God issues the command. You hold the power to obey. What is this key that will free you from negative anger and repressed hostility? Forgiveness.

Seeking Christ's forgiveness for sin is the place to begin. Then with the Holy Spirit working through you, seek out those you have injured and beg their forgiveness. Last, there may be people in your life who have asked forgiveness from you, and you have resisted. Why? Remember as Christ has forgiven you, so you are to forgive. Do you need Christ's forgiveness? Does someone need yours?

God blessed me with a wonderful father. I remember the nights when he came to my bed and knelt beside it, put his arm around me, and asked me to forgive him for being angry with me that day. I must confess if my long-suffering father were angry with me, I deserved his discipline. But his tender heart responded to God's warning, and he could not rest until he knew all was well. He made sure I was not hurting and building a wall of hostility and resentment. He never failed to add that he loved me. How comforting and precious that act of love was throughout my childhood. By seeking my forgiveness, he taught me how to forgive and keep close accounts.

Dr. Viscott says, "Be prepared to forgive. If you can't forgive, the relationship dies. If you insist on keeping the upper hand to punish the other person, you're still the captive of your own anger. To be free of anger means you're rid of both hurt and the desire for revenge. If you don't forgive, you carry a grudge, aligning sympathizers and dividing friendships. Forgiveness is the key to freedom, but it must come through sharing your pain."[13]

We are reminded in Jeremiah 51:56, "For the Lord is a God of retribution; he will repay in full." But in Luke 6:27 we are told to love our enemies, do good to those who hate us, bless those who curse us, and pray for those who mistreat us. Perhaps if we were obedient to the admonition of Jesus, our enemies would cease to be enemies.

God will repay in full but not how or when we think He should. It will be His way—the best way that the offender can learn from his offense.

Look at Luke 6:35. We are even to lend to our enemies without expecting anything returned. Keep reading. *Your reward will be great,* and *we will be children of the Most High.* Our Christlike actions will be a testimony to the world. How? By being kind to the ungrateful and wicked, we reflect the character of Christ. It also says we are to be merciful, just as Christ is merciful. Can you be merciful and still be unforgiving?

LET'S HEAR IT FOR RIGHTEOUS INDIGNATION!

Here is an encouraging word. Anger can be positive. Isn't that a relief? Frankl, Walesa, Linda, and the apostle Paul chose to allow God to make something good out of a bad situation. All the emotional energy was present, but was channeled in the right direction, and people were *benefiting* from their good anger.

In *From Here to Maturity,* David Augsburger writes, "Anger may be one of your greatest sources of inner power, one of your most important personal assets. To let it go unused is to rob yourself of much needed energy. . . . Anger can be a creative, constructive force that drives a man to achievements and accomplishments that would be utterly impossible without it."[14]

We need to exhibit more righteous indignation—anger—than we

do. We need to stand up for what is right, to admonish Christians who are disobeying God's Word, to demand justice where there is injustice, to protect our freedom to worship God, to defend the helpless and innocent, and to guard the sanctity of life. Our silence is condemning. God is not silent in His Word regarding sin and injustice. Neither should we be silent.

For too long, Christians have had a reputation for being passive. The time is always right for action. If we don't take action soon, it will be too late. Frankie Schaeffer clearly states, "We must once again commit ourselves to a robust view of truth. *Religious people must once again become involved in every area of life: politics, law, medicine, family life, education, science, the media, and the arts.* We must provide the example of an alternate way of living by placing our children and their care before our own ambitions and materialism."[15] A good place to begin is in our homes. Teach your children by example. See that they understand the principles of God's Word and learn to apply them to their lives.

Reach out into the neighborhood, schools, and city government. Study the issues and the candidates—VOTE. Work for the candidates who uphold God's Word. Support causes that protect life and liberty. With which talents and gifts has God blessed you? Use them to proclaim what is right and good and holy. Bring joy to God's heart by using what He has given you to bring honor and glory to Jesus Christ. Seek God's will as to how He would like you to use the emotion of anger He blessed you with. Yes—*blessed.* He gave it to you for a legitimate purpose. Ask Him what that purpose is. Then use anger correctly. A whole new world may be lying at your doorstep.

My husband Dan was a fiery-tempered redhead in his youth. Over the years, he has matured into a calm, level-headed adult. The emotional energy of anger, however, is still very much a part of him. It surfaced unexpectedly one night last winter as he was driving home from work.

Mirror Mirror

An older man in the lane next to Dan was trying to bump the white car just ahead. When the white car pulled in front of Dan, the angry driver tried to sideswipe it. Dan couldn't figure out why the one driver was so angry. The other driver was a young man, driving at the correct speed, obeying the laws. Everything seemed right to Dan.

Finally when they came to a red light, the angry man jumped out of his car, went around to the white car, and pulled the young man out. When the man's fists were raised, Dan's energy of anger propelled him out of his car and into the middle of the fracas. Quickly he grabbed both men, separated them, and told them in no uncertain terms that the fight was over. Surprised at the intervention, they got into their own cars; the light turned green, and everyone drove sensibly.

When Dan got home, he was embarrassed to tell me about his explosion of anger. He couldn't believe what he had done. Neither could I. It was so unlike my husband. I laughed as I hugged him. I was so proud of him for stopping a fight. His positive use of anger had produced good results.

Look for ways in everyday life to use your anger positively. Let's become involved in life around us and see that justice is honored. Determine to honor and glorify Jesus Christ with every emotion He has provided you, even anger. See how much good you can accomplish.

In the evening when God's glorious sunset spreads across the heavens, let it remind you to make peace where peace is needed. May you experience the blessing of sweet rest that forgiveness brings.

* * *

Love . . . is not rude, it is not self-seeking, it is not easily angered, it keeps no record of wrongs.

1 Corinthians 13:4–5

♡54

*   *   *

YOUR SPIRITUAL WORKOUT

1. What describer do you use to say you are angry?

2. Think for a moment how you generally react when angered. Do you blow up or simmer? Write a statement describing how you handle anger and what changes you need to make.

3. Considering Linda's problem again, would you have forgiven someone who murdered your loved one? Why or why not?

4. Remembering that physical ailments can be a result of unresolved anger, read Psalm 38 and list all the afflictions David mentions.

5. After some time of meditation, write out a prayer that expresses the kind of attitude you want to reveal if ever you should find yourself in Frankl's concentration camp, Walesa's prison, Linda's grief, or Paul's chains?

6. Describe briefly what this chapter has revealed to you about anger in your life. Then write out some ideas of ways you will determine to use your anger energy to help others and honor Jesus Christ.

NOTES

[1] Charles R. Swindoll, *Three Steps Forward Two Steps Back* (Nashville: Thomas Nelson, 1980).
[2] "Your Anger Is Not Your Enemy," *Charisma* (July 1984).
[3] Tim LaHaye and Bob Phillips, *Anger Is a Choice* (Grand Rapids: Zondervan, 1982).
[4] David Augsburger, *Caring Enough to Confront* (Ventura, Calif.: Regal, 1983).

[5] David Viscott, *The Viscott Method: A Revolutionary Program for Self-Analysis and Self-Understanding* (Boston: Houghton Mifflin, 1984).

[6] "Personality Profile," *This Week* (June 6, 1984).

[7] David A. Seamands, *Healing for Damaged Emotions* (Wheaton, Ill.: Victor, 1981).

[8] LaHaye and Phillips, *Anger is a Choice.*

[9] Seamands, *Healing for Damaged Emotions.*

[10] "Anger, the Burning Fuse of Hostility," *Moody Monthly* (November 1981).

[11] Viktor E. Frankl, *Man's Search for Meaning: An Introduction to Logotherapy* (New York: Pocket Books, 1973).

[12] "I Am Always Free," *Reader's Digest* (May 1984).

[13] Viscott, *The Viscott Method.*

[14] David Augsburger, *From Here to Maturity* (Wheaton, Ill.: Tyndale House, 1982).

[15] Franky Schaeffer, *A Time for Anger: The Myth of Neutrality* (Westchester, Ill.: Crossway Books, 1983).

Too Important to Ignore

Five of us were gulping our second cup of coffee. The lunch room clock ticked loudly, an incessant reminder to hurry back to work.

Norma, with her bright, vivacious personality, was once again the focus of attention. A few days ago she had bragged about a large income tax refund. "Just a little padding of expenses. Nothing illegal." Today she was exclaiming about the good fortune of her son. He had landed a job where he was paid cash under the table and was going to keep drawing his unemployment checks until his debts were caught up. "Why not? Everyone else does it," she reasoned.

I cringed. It wouldn't have bothered me so much if Norma didn't call herself a Christian.

On the way back to my desk, the apparent conflict between Norma's life style and her Christian testimony continued to bother me. As soon as there was an opportunity, I looked for a way to gently share a lesson I had painfully learned. So often in the past I had talked the talk of a Christian but hadn't walked the walk.

Mirror Mirror

I remember the time a friend had lovingly shown me the inconsistencies in my life and how poorly I was representing Christ. She shared an incident from the life of Alexander the Great, which gave me the insight I needed. It is told that the great conqueror once came across a young soldier who was sleeping on duty. He jerked the soldier awake and demanded his name. The startled youth replied, "It's Alexander, sir." Never would the young man forget his hero's reply. "Either change your ways or change your name."

And so it should be with a Christian. As we take the name of Christ, we need to change our ways.

TEMPTED TO IGNORE IT

Most of us would not readily admit we have a problem with stealing. In fact, most of us would just as soon skip over any chapter mentioning it. I certainly was tempted to ignore this subject. But it is right here in the Scripture we are studying. Ephesians 4:28 says:

> He who has been stealing must steal no longer, but must work, doing something useful with his own hands, that he may have something to share with those in need.

I tried to ignore the first part of the verse and zero in on the last phrase. Isn't that sometimes our tendency? We often pick out those parts of Scripture that feel more comfortable than others.

Even though I was inclined not to mention stealing, I knew neither God nor my publisher would be pleased. After all, "You shall not steal" is listed among the great commandments. How could I ignore it?

THE LITTLE FOXES

Part of the struggle I was having was caused by my perspective. I was only associating stealing with obvious infractions of the law and somehow I couldn't picture too many kleptomaniacs or Mafia members reading this book. It was then I remembered a quotation from the Song of Songs 2:15, which says it is "the little foxes that ruin the vineyards." Likewise, it is sometimes the little things that spoil our testimony for Christ.

Still not convinced we need to cover this concept? Then ask yourself if you are ever troubled with temptations similar to these: regularly returning a few minutes late from your coffee or lunch breaks; claiming your children are younger than they are to take advantage of lower admission prices; conducting personal business on company time; padding expense accounts; omitting income on government tax forms; using office supplies for personal use; ignoring the errors on bills that are to your advantage; using one-to-a-family specials more than once; passing messages through telephone operators at no cost to you.

This list is not meant to be all-inclusive. But if we look deep enough into our own circumstances, something will disturb our conscience. Or will it?

CAN YOUR CONSCIENCE BE YOUR GUIDE?

The U.S. Government has a Conscience Fund. Each year, hundreds of anonymous donations are received. One such donation was accompanied by a letter of explanation: "I have been unable to sleep lately because I misrepresented my income on last year's tax return. I am enclosing $75. If my sleep doesn't improve, I'll send the rest."

While one person's sleep is disturbed, thousands of others go about life not even aware or caring that they have become insensitive to living dishonestly.

Statistics on petty theft rise annually. Epidemics of shoplifting are reported across the country. McDonald's Corporation experiences slumps in profits when employees have pockets in their uniforms. The U.S.

Department of Justice estimates internal thefts cost American businesses between five and ten billion dollars *annually*. [1]

WHERE DOES IT BEGIN?

The government and corporations are having to deal with problems that begin in the home. Consider the following account:

When the boy was nine, his baseball skills lagged behind those in his age group. His father thought it would help if he played on a younger team and so altered the child's birth certificate. Another time, the son watched as a waitress brought back too much change. The father pocketed it with a brief comment that the prices were too high anyway.

While in high school, the same young man drove off the road and hit a telephone pole causing extensive damage to the front fender. Once again, Dad stepped in. He submitted insurance forms showing the damage was caused by a hit-and-run driver in a parking lot.

When the college years arrived, the family applied for and received a government grant based on financial need to help pay for college expenses. Part of their income had been omitted to qualify.

During the young man's second term at college, his parents received a heartbreaking phone call from the dean. Their son was being expelled because he had cheated on an exam. With total sincerity, the disillusioned father confronted his son and asked, "How could you bring this shame to our family after the good upbringing we gave you?"

The father did not realize how his actions had molded the boy's moral values. His conscience had barely shrugged as he had adjusted his standards to give both himself and his son what he thought was the best advantage.

The conscience by itself cannot be trusted. When it has been contaminated, abused, confused, seared, and defiled by the world, it is no longer responsive to God. The process of conscience destruction is subtle and gradual.

Our pastor explained with this illustration how the conscience can ignore the teaching of God. If we are in the same room with a dog barking out a warning, it would be difficult to ignore the danger. Even if we put the dog in the next room, we would still hear the warning and be bothered by it. But if the dog is put outside, the sound will become faint and easier to ignore. Finally if the dog is placed in a shed out back and all the doors and windows of the house are closed, we will no longer hear the barking. The dog will continue to issue an alert, but by placing ourselves far enough away, we can refuse to heed the warning.

So it is with our conscience. If we push the Word of God further and further out of the center of our lives, there will come a day when we are no longer sensitive to it. Then our own reasoning takes control, and we become capable of justifying all sorts of deceitfulness (Jeremiah 17:9). Only as we allow our conscience to be bathed in God's Word can it respond to the warnings of God.

God's admonition is "He who has been stealing must steal no longer." Can you still hear the warning? What is your response?

MOTIVATION FOR WORKING

Having determined to do away with any form of stealing, no matter how trifling it may seem, we must then entrust ourselves to God, who will meet all our needs. Along with the trust comes our obligation to work diligently and earn a living by honest means.

As we keenly examine our passage from Ephesians 4:28, we may be shocked to learn what God says our motivation should be for working. It is so we will have something to share with others. How absolutely foreign this motivation sounds to a generation weaned on the philosophy of putting self first.

Mirror Mirror

The emphasis on self has rapidly become widespread in our culture. As recent as ten years ago, a survey among students entering college showed their primary concern was for problems affecting the world. Today their chief concern is with problems affecting themselves. A decade ago the army enticed men into service with slogans, such as "Your country needs you." Now they appeal to self with the motto, "Be all you want to be."

While the philosophies of the world build to an ever louder crescendo of narcissism, God's emphasis throughout the ages remains the same. We are to put the needs of others before ourselves. This is reverse me-ism and reverse materialism. We are to make a living to give rather than to get.

SHARING VS. SELFISHNESS

The correct definition of "share" in context with Ephesians 4:28 is to distribute personally rather than to give something, as if by remote control, through some agent or official.

How far we have strayed from this concept. At one time, Americans were known for their sharing. There were the barn-raising parties, quilting bees, sharing food with the needy, and caring for the sick and elderly. Today we have become so isolated, we prefer giving our money by means of a check to some agency we have never seen. It is totally impersonal to us. We shy away from direct help where it can involve the touching of hands and the spoken word of encouragement. Gone are the front-porch days when neighbors spent their quiet afternoons or pleasant evenings expressing concerns and needs with each other. Has the government had to step in with their federal aid because we ceased to be a caring and sharing nation?

The theme of *selflessness* is not isolated to the Ephesians portion of

Scripture we are studying. It is one of the great doctrines of Christianity. We are to love and to give. God Himself is our example. "For God so loved the world that he gave his one and only son" (John 3:16).

Take time now to consider a mere handful of the many Scriptures that emphasize this great theme. You will see that for the Christian selfless giving is not a choice. It is a *mandate.*

> A new commandment I give you: Love one another. As I have loved you, so you must love one another. All men will know that you are my disciples if you love one another (John 13:34–35).

> We who are strong ought to bear with the failings of the weak and not to please ourselves. Each of us should please his neighbor for his good, to build him up (Romans 15:1–2).

> Do nothing out of selfish ambition or vain conceit, but in humility consider others better than yourselves. Each of you should look not only to your own interests, but also to the interests of others (Philippians 2:3–4).

> This is how we know what love is: Jesus Christ laid down his life for us. And we ought to lay down our lives for our brothers. If anyone has material possessions and sees his brother in need but has no pity on him, how can the love of God be in him? (1 John 3:16–17).

Now wait a minute. Did you really consider these verses? Go back and read them again carefully, word for word. Read as though you were seeing them for the first time. Meditate and ask God to brand your heart with His message.

THE TIME OF OUR LIVES

As we think about the needs of others, the ways to respond are as varied as the circumstances. Much is discussed throughout this book that will help you respond effectively. Giving of our money and possessions is only one way. Perhaps it is the easiest way. To give of ourselves and our time is the most costly and most difficult.

Time is a limited resource; it can be spent only once. If wasted, it cannot be redeemed. Daily we each receive the same twenty-four hours. It matters not if we are great or small, rich or poor, young or old. The measure is the same.

So often we recite, "This is the first day of the rest of my life." I wonder how differently we would use the time if we knew it were the last day of the rest of our lives?

Chuck Swindoll relates a story of how he was painfully reminded of the reality that life is a passing thing.

> I arrived at my office unusually early this morning. Things were quiet, the sky was heavy and overcast, a normal California fall morning. My mind was on my schedule as I fumbled with the keys. In standard Swindoll fashion I pushed the door wide open in a hurry—only to be stopped dead in my tracks. A chill went up my back as I peered into the spooky study. The light switch is across the room, so I stood there at the door staring at the most startling reminder of reality imaginable! In the middle of the floor, sitting on rollers, was a *casket* . . . with a wilted spray of flowers on top alongside a picture of ME![2]

It took a few moments for him to realize this was the result of a practical joke. In those few moments, he was given a fresh perspective on the transitory state of life.

Each day is given as a gift from God. It is not a thing to take for granted. It is not a thing that is our right. It is not a thing to possess. We are accountable to God for how we use the treasure of time. Would it be too bold or too presumptuous to say that if we do not love, if we do not give, or if we hoard all for ourselves, we have stolen from the very hand of God?

HOW LONG?

There is a story of a missionary doctor who had spent forty years of his life ministering in the primitive villages of Africa. Finally, he decided to retire. He wired ahead that he would be returning by ship and gave the date and time of his arrival.

As he was crossing the Atlantic, he thought back over all the years he had spent helping to heal the people of Africa, both physically and spiritually. Then his thoughts raced ahead to the grand homecoming he knew awaited him in America because he had not been home in all forty years.

As the ship pulled into port, the old man's heart swelled with pride as he saw the homecoming that had been prepared. A great crowd of people had gathered, and there was a huge banner saying, "Welcome Home." As the man stepped off the ship onto the dock and awaited a great ovation, his heart sank. Suddenly he realized the people had not gathered to pay tribute to him but to a movie star who had been aboard the same ship.

He waited in anguish with his heart breaking. No one had come to welcome him home. As the crowd disbursed, the old man was left waiting alone. Tilting his face heavenward, he spoke these words, "Oh God, after giving all those years of my life to my fellow man, was it too much to ask that one person—just one person—be here to welcome me as I came back home?"

In the quietness of his heart, he seemed to hear the voice of God whisper to him, "You're not home yet. When you come home to me, you will be welcomed."[3]

The days turn into weeks; the weeks into months; the months into years. When all of our tomorrows have become yesterdays, will we still be asked to love and give? Yes! We must continue the vigil. As each day is given, we must choose to live it in a way that brings honor to the name of Christ.

The time is coming when we will cross the threshold from this world into heaven. Then there will be a great celebration. What a homecoming it will be!

* * *

Only one life, 'twill soon be past.
Only what's done for Christ will last.

* * *

YOUR SPIRITUAL WORKOUT

1. Ask the Lord to reveal to you areas in your own life that are inconsistent or that bring dishonor to His name. How can 1 Corinthians 10:13 help you in overcoming these problems?

2. Can you think of other situations not mentioned in this chapter where people tend to tolerate actions that, under closer scrutiny, steal from government organizations, businesses, or people?

3. Take time to review how you have spent your days this past week. What percentage of time was used meeting the needs of others? Is this a good balance? How can you improve?

4. Now look at your calendar for the next few weeks. How can you plan ahead to allow time for helping others?

5. Be creative!
   a. Think of someone you have never helped before. What can you do for this person?
   b. Plan something new and different for someone you frequently help. What can you do this week?

6. For one week keep a journal recording at the end of the day the times you caught yourself either feeling or acting selfishly. Make a note telling why you felt the way you did. Analyze those feelings and attitudes and ask God to help you put a watch on your heart, so you may check the attitude or action before it becomes a habit.

NOTES

[1] "The Inside Job," *Northwest Magazine* (March 11, 1984):

[2] Charles R. Swindoll, *Growing Strong in the Seasons of Life* (Portland, Oreg.: Multnomah, 1983).

[3] Transcript of speech by Michael Broome, "How to Be a Liver of Life and Not a Gallbladder," delivered at COSA Convention, Seaside, Oregon, on June 23, 1984.

Heart Language

How beautiful is your tongue?
Or haven't you ever really considered your tongue in terms of its attractiveness?
You don't go on shopping trips for it.
You don't have a weekly appointment at the tongue beautician.
Avon and Revlon don't sell cosmetics for it.
You don't have to diet to get it back in shape.
Men don't ogle it or whistle at it or write poems about it.[1]

We have to admit a lot of time and effort is spent making ourselves attractive. We perm the top of our head and paint the tips of our toes. We moisturize, diet, exercise, clothe, jewel, and pamper ourselves. But there is one part we seldom think about beautifying—the tongue.

Why should we give attention to this definitely unattractive member of our bodies? After all, it is only a small chunk of muscle and nerves that helps us taste, chew, and pick food from between our teeth. Or is it?

The tongue can also bring a timely word of encouragement or deliver an agonizing blow of ridicule. It can convey words of healing and comfort or lash out in anger and destruction. It can praise or it can criticize. More than anything else, the tongue can make a plain person beautiful or make an outwardly beautiful person ugly.[2]

BEAUTY CARE BEGINS IN THE HEART

Imagine for a moment an exquisite silver goblet inlaid with gold, resting on an ornate tray and carried carefully by a servant. All who observe think the goblet is filled with a succulent beverage for the master. Imagine the shock when the servant stumbles and the goblet tips, spilling out a contaminated, slimy liquid with a putrid odor. Suddenly the offensive contents command our attention, and the illusion of beauty has been defiled.

The same is true for us. We can carefully guard our speech for a time but eventually we stumble. Our true character is then revealed as ". . . out of the overflow of the heart the mouth speaks" (Matthew 12:34). It is for this reason that beauty care for the tongue must begin with the heart.

WHAT IS THE HEART?

One morning in Sunday School, a young preschooler watched as his older friend told his teacher, "I asked Jesus into my heart last night." The teacher's reaction included joyful exclamations, hugs, an announcement to the rest of the class, and even a special song.

Later that afternoon, the child who had watched all this happen tugged at his mother's elbow and whispered, "I asked Jesus into my heart." The mother did not want to deny the faith of her young child but felt she needed to probe further to see if he understood what he had expressed.

The boy stood patiently waiting for her response, as his foot toyed with a loosened shoestring on his tennis shoe. With her arm gently around his shoulder, she lowered herself to his height and asked him to tell her how Jesus had come into his heart. His eyes opened wide, and his face became intense with the seriousness of the moment. The words tumbled out. "Well, Mom, I just opened my mouth, and he crawled right in."

It was with patience and diligence that the mother began to teach her young man about the heart. His comprehension did not happen in a moment but was the result of weeks and months of preparation. Then came the glorious day when, once again, the boy shared that he had received Jesus into his heart as his personal Savior. This time he had faith *and* understanding.

Jerry Bridges explains,

> Heart, in Scripture, is used in various ways. Sometimes it means our reason or understanding, sometimes our affections and emotions, and sometimes our will. Generally it denotes the whole soul of man and all its faculties, not individually, but as they all work together in doing good or evil. The mind as it reasons, discerns, and judges; the emotions as they like or dislike; the conscience as it determines and warns; and the will as it chooses or refuses—all are together called the heart.[3]

WHERE DO WE BEGIN?

How do we reach the heart to beautify the tongue? We have already seen in the illustration of the silver goblet that any surface effort to control our speech will eventually end in disaster. Almost all of the third chapter of James expounds the power of the tongue and the futility of our trying to tame it by our own strength. The only result we can expect from our effort is failure.

How then do we beautify the tongue? We do it by beautifying the heart. My friend Carol used the following diagram to illustrate the necessity of beginning with the heart.

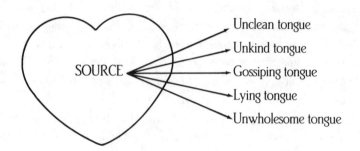

BEAUTY CARE OF THE HEART

Beautification of the heart can only occur as we place ourselves under the care of God—the Heart Beautifier. He begins with a thorough cleansing as we confess and repent our sin and deceitfulness (I John 1:9; Jeremiah 17:9). As we learned in chapter 2, He continues this purging on a regular basis when we ask Him to search our hearts and thoughts for hurtful ways (Psalm 139:23–24).

Once our heart has been cleansed, we open the door to making God's principles a priority in our lives. David instructs us by his example in Psalm 119 to hide God's Word in our heart to keep us from sin. In addition to knowing it, we must apply it daily in real-life situations and use it as a sentinel to guard our minds against the pollution of the world. It is the Word of God that judges the thoughts and attitudes of the heart (Hebrews 4:12).

Beautification of the heart does not happen all at once. It is an ongoing process. Only as we continue to submit to God and His teachings will the meditation of our heart and the words of our mouth be pleasing to Him (Psalm 19:14).

As our heart is beautified, so is the tongue. Then we are able to fulfill God's desire for our speech as expressed in Ephesians 4:29, "Do not let any unwholesome talk come out of your mouths, but only what is helpful for building others up according to their needs, that it may benefit those who listen.''

Unwholesome talk encompasses a great variety of offensive communication. Three of the most toxic areas are criticism, slander, and malice.

FAST FROM NEGATIVE

Catherine Marshall has related some startling discoveries after experimenting with a one-day fast—not from food, but from criticism.

The first half of the day she felt void. This was especially apparent when she had lunch with her husband and his secretary. Since most of the topics of conversation centered around circumstances, issues, laws, and policies where she normally would tend to be critical, she remained silent. She was quite surprised to observe her comments were not missed.

It was not until midafternoon that she began to see what her criticism fast was accomplishing. Fresh creative ideas started to flow, having previously been stifled by a critical nature. Her prayers for someone who had become sidetracked in his life shifted from a negative to a specific, positive vision. She was inspired to write a letter of love and appreciation and send it to a friend. She was motivated to ask forgiveness from a son and to release him to receive guidance from God rather than from her.

In the evening, she pondered the lessons she had learned, and they were amazing. She continues to experiment with days of fasting from criticism as she has realized how a negative attitude blocks the positive attributes of the Spirit of God—love, good will, mercy, and understanding.[4]

FEAST ON THE POSITIVE

If we are to fast from words that tear others down, then we should feast on those that build them up. One lady I know has posted a brightly colored card on her refrigerator with the equation $7 = 1$ in bold print. It is a reminder to her to reinforce her children with praise. She once read that it takes seven positive statements to counteract the effects of one negative comment.

In his excellent book *Hide or Seek,* Dr. James Dobson encourages statements and actions that convince a child he is greatly loved and respected. But remembering that we are to be genuine and selective in our compliments, Dr. Dobson cautions against inflationary praise.

> It is helpful to distinguish between the concepts of flattery vs. praise. Flattery is unearned. It is what Grandma says when she comes for a visit: "Oh, look at my beautiful little girl! You're getting prettier each day. I'll bet you'll have to beat the boys off with a club when you get to be a teenager!" Or "My what a smart boy you are." Flattery occurs when you heap compliments upon the child for something he did not achieve.
>
> Praise, on the other hand, is used to reinforce positive, constructive behavior. It should be highly specific rather than general. "You've been a good boy . . ." is unsatisfactory. "I like the way you kept your room straight today" is better. Parents should always watch for opportunities to offer genuine, well-deserved praise to their children, while avoiding empty flattery.[5]

Affirmation is as important to the adult as it is to the child. Just this week, I received a letter from a friend in California who related her experience to me.

A small group of ladies had been close friends for ten years. They first met in a neighborhood Bible study. Although some had moved away and others had new commitments, they still met once each year for a special reunion.

Heart Language

This year the celebration was exceptional. Acts of appreciation and encouragement were in abundance. When their time together drew to a close, everyone was reluctant to leave.

Finally as the good-bys were about to begin, one in the group rose from her chair and explained she had something more to share. With tears and halting speech, she told her dear friends that her marriage of thirty years had fallen apart. She was now separated and seeking a divorce. As she finished, she sat down, crumpled in soul and spirit.

For a moment there was only silence, and then a precious lady spoke softly, "Now is not the time to give advice or to form judgments. Now is the time for affirmation. We will go around the table, not in order, but each as they wish will take their turn. Let's all share something we love and appreciate about our friend as a person."

Can you imagine the ministry and healing that took place as each spoke words from her own heart to help mend the broken heart of another? Praise and affirmation are only two entrees of the feast necessary to meet the needs of others. Encouragement is another.

SUPPLY AND DEMAND

One of the best-selling books on the Christian market is a small volume about encouragement.[6] One of the reasons it sells so well is that there is an ample supply of people needing encouragement and a shortage of encouragers.

No matter how faithful and no matter how earnest a Christian is, there will be times of spiritual dryness. In almost every autobiography of a great Christian, there is a chapter where the author identifies with the psalmist when he cried out, "Why art thou cast down, O my soul?" (Psalm 42:5, 11 KJV).

Equipped with a shepherd's experience, author Phillip Keller draws a parallel between the cry of David and the care of sheep. He explains when a sheep is cast down, it has turned over on its back and no matter how frantically it struggles, it is unable to get back on its feet. Unless someone comes to its assistance, the sheep will die.[7] It is not only the weak and frail sheep that get cast down. Often it is the healthiest and strongest.

And so it is with Christians. Even though we are mature in our walk with the Lord, our souls get cast down and no matter how we struggle, we cannot seem to get up on our own.

It is then we need others to come along and help. We need those who will understand, those who will help without criticism, those who will speak words of encouragement and hope.

HEART LANGUAGE

Caring words that flow from a heart submitted to God reach out and meet the needs of others in a myriad of ways. Not only is there a necessity for praise, affirmation, and encouragement, but also there is much to be done in listening, in sharing the message of salvation, and in bringing hope where the way seems hopeless. Note how Joe Bayly portrayed comfort after losing three precious children:

> I was sitting torn by grief. Someone came and talked to me of God's dealings, of why it happened, of hope beyond the grave. He talked constantly. He said things I knew were true.
>
> I was unmoved, except to wish he'd go away. He finally did.
>
> Another came and sat beside me. He didn't talk. He didn't ask me leading questions. He just sat beside me for an hour and more, listened when I said something, answered briefly, prayed simply, left.
>
> I was moved. I was comforted. I hated to see him go.[8]

Words are a primary part of heart language. And yet, sometimes it is in quietness that the heart speaks the loudest.

Heart Language

* * *

A word aptly spoken is like apples of gold in settings of silver.

Proverbs 25:11

* * *

YOUR SPIRITUAL WORKOUT

1. Look up these additional verses concerning speaking. Choose one that you like best and write a paragraph about how to apply it to your own life. Psalm 19:14; Matthew 12:34–37; Romans 10:9–10; James 3:1–12.

2. How would you help a young child understand the term Heart as it is used in Scripture?

3. When you are angry or upset, are there words that spill out that you regret? Review the section "Beauty Care of the Heart." List the actions you should take.

4. Think of recent conversations with your spouse, children, parents, or friends. Consider if you used words to build up or to tear down. What suggestions can you think of for improvement?

5. Write out a few phrases that would be genuine compliments, rather than flattery, for a particular person you want to affirm.

6. Take time now to pray for someone who needs encouragement. Along with the prayer, what can you do to uplift that person today?

NOTES

[1] LeRoy Koopman, *Beauty Care for the Tongue* (Grand Rapids: Zondervan, 1972).

[2] Ibid., adapted from pages 7–8.

[3] Adapted from the definition of the heart by the Puritan John Owen in his treatise *Indwelling Sin* (1656) as it appears in *Temptation and Sin* (Evansville, Ind.: Sovereign Grace Books Club, rep. ed., 1958) as quoted in Jerry Bridges, *The Pursuit of Holiness* (Colorado Springs: Navpress, 1978).

[4] "My Experiment With Fault-finding," *Guideposts* vol. 38 no. 1 (March 1983).

[5] James C. Dobson, *Hide or Seek* (Old Tappan, N.J.: Fleming H. Revell, 1974).

[6] Charles R. Swindoll, *Encourage Me* (Portland, Ore.: Multnomah, 1983).

[7] Phillip Keller, *A Shepherd Looks at Psalm 23* (Grand Rapids: Zondervan, 1970).

[8] Joseph T. Bayly, *The Last Thing We Talk About*, rev. ed. (Elgin, Ill.: David C. Cook, 1973), quoted in Charles R. Swindoll, *Growing Strong in the Seasons of Life* (Portland, Ore.: Multnomah, 1983).

The Other Side Of Heart Language

Excitedly our Bible study teacher hurried to the platform and immediately began her lecture with this exclamation, "Wait until I tell you the breathtaking news I just heard!" Instantly she had our total attention. A short pause followed, then she smiled. "That's communication," she said.

Next she waved frantically and motioned with her hand as if calling someone over to her. Again her action was followed with the brief statement, "That's communication."

Abruptly she changed position and stood with arms folded firmly in front of her, an impatient scowl spreading from brow to chin. Again she made the short declaration about communication. With the ease of a mime, her expression changed to a radiant smile as she walked to one of the ladies in the audience and embraced her with a warm, friendly hug. "That's communication."

Back on the platform, she stood motionless facing the audience. There was a long, silent pause. Then she leaned forward and continued to fix her eyes intently on us. Slowly she nodded her head in an expression of understanding and quietly spoke the words, "That's communication." Listening is the unheard side of communication.

A COMPLIMENT?

Has anyone ever complimented you by telling you what a wonderful conversationalist you are? Perhaps when you are around, there is never a lull in the conversation. People enjoy your clever, quick retorts. You are the envy of some of your quieter friends.

Before spending too much time basking in this praise, let's see what God's Word has to say. Being of a somewhat outgoing temperament, I used to pride myself in never being at a loss for words. One day James 1:19 reached out and grabbed me by the tongue. "Take note of this: Everyone should be quick to listen, slow to speak. . . ."

The beginning phrase is an attention-getter, which alerts us to the message that follows. We are to be *quick* to listen and *slow* to speak. Most of us are just the opposite: motor-mouths who are quick to speak and slow to hear.

This verse from the book of James is my favorite about listening, but there are many other references throughout the Bible. They are nestled among great passages having to do with wisdom, counsel, and understanding. Many are in the New Testament, and Christ Himself often concluded His teachings with the words, "He who has ears, let him hear."

VALUE OF LISTENING

There are two goals we want to consider. The first is to emphasize the importance of listening, and the second is to share some ways to improve listening skills. It has already been mentioned that there are numerous Bible passages that deal with this subject. That in itself documents its importance.

The Other Side Of Heart Language

An observation made by David Augsburger in his book *Caring Enough to Hear* gives a totally different perspective.

> From birth to death, listening and being listened to is the breath of our emotional life.
>
> The rhythmic sound of the mother's heartbeat provides the first sensory stimulation an infant receives. At birth, loud noises and falling are the two primal fears. Gentle sounds and warm enveloping arms are the first sources of security. Listening remains the basic channel for sensing emotions and reading the feeling tone between oneself and another all throughout the stages of life. It is usually the last sense to remain when a stroke cuts off sight, speech, and smell. Hearing communicates deep feeling to the heart of a person at any age.[1]

Another dimension to the value of listening is its ministry. Listening is unselfish because the needs of the other person are placed first. Listening demonstrates that you care and that you think someone is worthwhile. When you listen, really listen, you are honoring, valuing, and respecting that person. "Being heard is so closely related to being loved, that for the average person they are almost indistinguishable."[2]

The story is told of the mother who came home after a long hard day. Her little girl ran out of the house to greet her. "Mommy, Mommy, wait until I tell you what happened today." After listening to a few sentences, the mother responded by indicating the rest could wait as she needed to get dinner started. During the meal, the phone rang, then other family members' stories were longer and louder than the little girl's. Once again she tried after the kitchen was cleaned and the brother's homework questions were answered, but then it was time for her to get ready for bed.

The mom came to tuck her little girl in and quickly listened to her prayers. As she bent down to tousle the little one's curls and to kiss her soft cheek, the child looked up and asked, "Mommy, do you really love me even if you don't have time to listen to me?"

On his "Insight for Living" radio program, Chuck Swindoll explained the equation of love and listening this way: "What you do when you listen is put your hand quietly on the other one's life and feel gently along the rim of his soul until you come to a crack or some frustration, some problem, or anguish that you sense, though he may not even be conscious of it. And as you are listening, you are loving the person. You are accepting him just as he is."

As we move into the practical side of listening, we must guard against losing the ministry dimension. Therefore as we examine listening techniques, let us constantly be aware that we are learning to speak love as we listen. Listening is unspoken heart language.

HOW ARE YOUR LISTENING SKILLS?

Following is a quiz about ten traits that may prevent you from being a good listener. Score yourself on a scale from one to ten as you review the list. Give yourself a low score if you frequently display the poor listening habit. Rate yourself high for each question that seldom applies to you. Score yourself in the middle of the scale if your answer is Sometimes. When you finish, add up your total points for the quiz.

HOW ARE YOUR LISTENING SKILLS?

ALWAYS		USUALLY		SOMETIMES		SELDOM		NEVER	
1	2	3	4	5	6	7	8	9	10

1. Do your thoughts take side excursions when someone else is speaking?

2. Do you try to make people think you are listening when you are not?

3. Do you wait impatiently for the other person to finish so you can have a turn to speak?

4. Do you stop listening when the subject matter gets difficult?

5. Do you become easily distracted by other influences, such as television, someone else's conversation, or other activities?

6. Do you try to second-guess the speaker and either cut him off and finish the sentence or interrupt his idea before he is finished?

7. Do people consider you quick to speak rather than quick to listen?

8. Do you offer a solution in such a hurry, that you have not heard the whole problem?

9. Do you become defensive or negative when someone has a different viewpoint than you have or when someone is speaking about a problem area in your life?

10. Do you listen only for what you want to hear?

Did you score 100? 90? 80? If you are like most of us, your score is low enough to indicate that help is needed to improve your listening habits. Some good resources for comprehensive aid are listed in the Recommended Reading section of this book. For the rest of this chapter, we will attempt a minicourse.

WHEN ARE YOU A POOR LISTENER?

In Norman Wakefield's book *Listening*, he uses this story from a "Dennis the Menace" cartoon to help answer when we are poor listeners:

> Dennis goes to Mr. Wilson, his neighbor, who is reading the newspaper and gives him a warm "Hello, Mr. Wilson." No response. Dennis speaks a little louder. "Hello, Mr. Wilson." Still no response. Finally, Dennis blasts forth with "HELLO, MR. WILSON!" No answer. Dennis turns to leave and in a normal voice says, "Well, then, goodbye, Mr. Wilson." Mr. Wilson replies, "Goodbye, Dennis." As he walks out the door, Dennis remarks, "There's nothing wrong with his hearing, but his listening's not so good."[3]

Mr. Wilson had several obstacles that prevented him from listening to Dennis: disinterest, disruption, preoccupation, and even prejudice. How could this little guy with the cowlick have anything worthwhile to say?

Evaluate situations in your home, your church, your business, and your neighborhood. What are some of the obstacles that keep you from being a good listener?

Some of mine would include time pressures, fatigue, wanting my turn to talk, and becoming bored with someone who is uninteresting or long-winded. I also must guard against becoming defensive when given constructive criticism or when confronted with a different viewpoint. At times, I have internal distractions, such as my own worries or problems. External distractions are more controllable for me now, but I still remember constant interruptions when the children were younger.

REMOVE OBSTACLES

Not all of us are effective listeners by nature, but this skill can be learned. We must begin by conscientiously evaluating when and why we are not listening with interest to someone. Once this cause is identified, we must remove the obstacle or circumvent it.

To do so, determine who is in control of the obstacle. If I am defensive about what is being said, I am in control. When the obstacle is controlled by me, I must choose to remove it before I can fully listen. If it is controlled by someone else, I must decide to go beyond the obstacle and listen in spite of it.[4]

CONCENTRATE

Having disposed of the obstacles, we can begin listening with the intent to minister to the other person. We must use our full faculties to concentrate on the person speaking. We need to show this concentration with eye contact, facial expression, body language, and even touch.

Many times my kitchen table will be the place where friends gather to talk over concerns. After they go home, my shoulders ache from leaning forward and listening with absolute intensity.

Demonstrating concentration helps the person speaking to express himself better. This is true in one-on-one conversations, small groups, and even very large audiences. Nothing is more encouraging to a speaker or pastor than to have people in the audience interacting. Eye contact, a smile, a nod of agreement, leaning forward with interest—all help the speaker. Many times after giving a lecture, I will seek out members of the audience and personally thank them for encouraging me by being such wonderful listeners.

SHOW ACCEPTANCE

This step in the listening process simply means to listen without judgment. Acknowledge that the other person has a right to say what he feels. This, of course, does not mean our children are allowed to speak disrespectfully or that we should accept abusive language. Nevertheless, listening with acceptance does greatly improve conversation with teenagers and others who have differing viewpoints. It is important to realize that acceptance is *not* agreement. It is trying to understand how the other person feels.

GIVE FEEDBACK

The need for feedback is illustrated in this frustrated statement:

> I know you think you understand what you thought I said, but I'm not sure you are aware that what you heard is not what I meant.

We must use feedback to clarify what the other person meant. We can do this in a variety of ways: Ask questions, summarize, and reflect back not only words but emotions or feelings expressed by the speaker. Statements might include something like these examples: "You seem to be very discouraged," or "I understand you feel angry when I do that."

Now go back and review the Listening Skills Quiz. Consider how your answers would change if you applied the four-step process you have learned in our minicourse:

1. Remove obstacles
2. Concentrate
3. Show acceptance
4. Give feedback

It's likely your score will reach 100 when applying these principles.

CARE VS. CURE

Even when we attempt to apply all of the above steps for listening, communication can still be short-circuited by a tendency to try to cure people's problems for them. Sometimes we are too quick to moralize, criticize, instruct, or offer advice. If we allow the full process of communication to take place, especially the feedback step, many times the person will be led to his own problem solving and decision making.

Instead of listening only with cure in mind, we need to listen with care. This involves listening deeply. Try to experience life from the speaker's viewpoint. Listen to the problem, the hurt, the joy with all your being. Listening with care is indeed another side of heart language.[5]

LISTEN TO GOD

No discussion about listening would be complete without a segment concerning the necessity of listening to God. Too many times our communication with God is a one-sided conversation.

Can you imagine calling a friend on the telephone, sharing all your joys and cares, then abruptly plopping down the receiver without waiting for a response? If we are going to do that, we might as well stand in an empty room and voice our concerns to the ceiling. Unfortunately, too many Christians view their prayer life as voicing concerns to an empty room.

To hear God, we can use our same four basic principles. We must remove obstacles or distractions. We must give God our full concentration. We must listen with acceptance. And we must make certain we fully understand the intent of His words.

We must not forget God is there and he is not silent. His Holy Word and His Holy Spirit work together to communicate His truth personally to us.

God has chosen to reveal His heart to us. He has shared His plans and hopes; He takes us into His confidence. Can we grasp this privilege?

We would be thrilled to have an audience with the President of the United States, the Queen of England, the Pope, or some other great dignitary. Yet somehow we fail to comprehend the awesome privilege of having an audience with the almighty living God. We have been invited to come boldly to His throne of grace where we can share our deepest concerns with our heavenly Father and find help in times of need.

There are times in my prayer life that I imagine myself entering a great and mighty throne room. I come with boldness and confidence because it belongs to my Father and He has invited me there. He is so glad to see me. It is because of His response that I have the faith and trust of a little child. I rush into His open arms and begin to tell Him my joys, my sorrows, and my cares. He is so delighted with me. He rejoices with my joy. He gives me wise counsel. He holds me close and comforts me.

It is in His presence that I am still. It is here that I listen. And the heart language I hear is God's.

* * *

His voice is often just a whisper.
A moment when He quietly touches your heart.[6]

* * *

YOUR SPIRITUAL WORKOUT

1. Reread some of the obstacles suggested on page 84. What can you add to the suggestions from your own experience?

2. Review your answers to the Listening Skills Quiz. Which of these four basic principles for better listening would help you most to overcome the negative traits on the quiz?
   a. Remove obstacles
   b. Concentrate
   c. Show acceptance
   d. Give feedback

3. Evaluate your personal devotion time with God by considering the four basic principles of listening listed above. How can you improve your listening skills with God?

4. List some words that describe how you feel when you realize that someone is not really listening to you.

5. Now list some words that describe how you feel when you know someone is listening carefully and fully understands what you are trying to express.

6. Pray about a listening ministry the Lord may give you. Write out some steps to help you begin. Mark on your calendar to help you see how you're progressing month by month.

NOTES

[1] David Augsburger, *Caring Enough to Hear and Be Heard* (Ventura, Calif.: Regal, 1982).
[2] Ibid.
[3] Norman Wakefield, *Listening: A Christian's Guide to Loving Relationships* (Waco: Word Books, 1981).
[4] Ibid.
[5] For further discussion of the concept of listening with care, see Augsburger, *Caring Enough to Hear and Be Heard,* 166.
[6] Phyllis Hobe, ed., *Fragile Moments . . . When God Speaks in Whispers* (Old Tappan, N.J.: Fleming H. Revell, 1980).

The Essence of God

Recently I was involved in a conversation with a derelict on skid row. In former visits with him, he told me he knew Christ personally. Yet on this day, his unwholesome remarks cut me to the marrow of my being.

Just a week before that conversation, I was in a home attending a reception for educators. A group of us were enjoying a delightful conversation with the hostess. She was a very attractive, smartly dressed, successful professional. Suddenly her clever repartee attacked the God I love, and her words sliced through me like a white-hot sword. My smile faded while others in our circle laughed. Stunned, I walked away. Again unwholesome talk had assaulted me.

Unwholesome conversation is corrupt and morally harmful to the mind. It is of itself rotten and spreads rottenness around. Included in this rottenness is not only bad language but also malicious gossip and slander as well. On the one hand was the derelict; on the other the professional. They were different as far as education, social status, and responsibility but in the same class as far as their manner of conversation.

I was more grieved with the derelict for he claimed to be a child of God. It occurred to me that if *I* were grieved, how much more so the Holy Spirit. Though the educator disappointed me, she did not claim to be God's child. Therefore, the Holy Spirit was not within her. But if the derelict were a child of God, as he claimed he was, then the Holy Spirit resided in him and was sorely grieved beyond any grief we can ever experience.

There are many ways of bringing sorrow to the Holy Spirit, but in Ephesians 4:29–30, Paul continues addressing the issue of unwholesome conversation after the conjunction "and." Paul is encouraging us to think still deeper.

"Do not let *any* unwholesome talk come out of your mouths . . . *and* do not grieve the Holy Spirit of God, with whom you were sealed for the day of redemption" (italics mine). The gravity of the problem of unwholesome speech is seen in the use of the full title Holy Spirit of God. Do not grieve the Holy Spirit with unholy talk.

To grieve is to give pain of mind to someone, to afflict, to cause distress or to injure. It's a serious thing to give pain of mind to the Holy Spirit of God. But we often glibly talk without thought or concern as to what our words are doing to either the listener or the Holy Spirit. If we practiced the mental awareness of God while standing in our circle of conversation, wouldn't it help to keep us from yielding to the temptation of unwholesome talk? If only we could grasp the seriousness of this issue.

Not only does God the Holy Spirit hear our every word, but He also knows what we're going to say before we have even given it thought! In giving us free will, He took the known risk of our making wrong decisions and committing unrighteous acts. It is by the exercising of our will that we do right or wrong, either grieve or bring glory.

The resulting actions of our exercised will always reveal the condition of our inner being. We may all look different on the outside but from inside we find that too many look alike. No wonder Christ warned us about judging others. Although there was no comparison in outward appearance between the derelict and the educator, their mouths revealed that the contents of their hearts were evil. From within, they looked alike.

WHAT DOES MAKE THE DIFFERENCE?

What sets a birthday cake apart from any other cake? It's the candles. The lit candles light up the face of the honored one when the cake is placed before him. What sets a Christian apart from others in the world? It is the Holy Spirit of God. We become His dwelling place the moment we accept Christ's forgiveness of our sins. He takes up residency within us and begins to perform the work given Him by God. It is the Holy Spirit in us that makes the difference. He lights up our lives.

When I was a girl scout in grade school, the Girl Scout Council of our city staged an annual lantern parade. Every girl scout in the city created a lantern that would be judged for originality and beauty.

At sundown, we lit our lanterns and lined up to parade before the townspeople. We walked up one side of the boulevard and down the other in single file so the delicate patterns could best be seen. People lined the street to watch as the lit lanterns displayed the unique art work of each girl. The lanterns were just so much cardboard, cellophane, and paint until the flashlights shone inside. Then the beautiful patterns of each lantern were revealed. No longer did we see the cardboard and paint, only the lovely colors of the cellophaned designs illumined.

And that is how it is with each human being. As a person accepts Christ as Savior, the Holy Spirit of God enters his life never to leave. He illuminates the unique design God has created in each of us. Then He places us in a strategic position where His new creation, made beautiful by the presence of His Light within, may be seen. That design is the special way God wants to work out His love to others through us so that His beloved Son might be seen in the darkness of the world around us.

As we shine for Him, the world will feel the love and warmth radiating from the beauty of Christ within us.

STRUGGLE VS. STRENGTH

Are you allowing the Holy Spirit to accomplish His work? Or does the assertive self-will demand its rights? Romans 8:8 says if we are controlled by our sinful nature we cannot please God. Then verses 10 and 11 say, "But if Christ is in you, your body is dead because of sin, yet your spirit is alive because of righteousness. And if the Spirit of Him who raised Jesus from the dead is living in you, he who raised Christ from the dead will also give life to your mortal bodies through his Spirit, who lives in you."

Paul goes on to share that since the Spirit of God is living in us, we have an obligation to put to death the misdeeds of the body because if we are led by the Spirit of God (Romans 8:16), believing in Christ has already put the flesh—our old nature—to death. "Those who belong to Christ Jesus have crucified the sinful nature with its passions and desires. Since we live by the Spirit, let us keep in step with the Spirit" (Galatians 5:24–25).

Dear ones, we are *dead* to sin's power because we have been made *alive* in Christ Jesus. We have been made new from within, and the FOR SALE sign has been torn down and replaced with a new sign saying, BOUGHT BY JESUS CHRIST. At the moment of purchase, the Holy Spirit moved in and began renovating *His*, no longer our, new dwelling. New power that is continuously available replaces the old, burned-out life.

Are you using that power? If you are fretting, struggling, and ridden with anxiety, then you are not accepting the marvelous power of the Holy Spirit in your life. Perhaps you are like the African national helping a missionary do her housework. The missionary had taught her the week before how to use the old wringer washer. When it was time to do the laundry again, the African was allowed to handle it by herself. When the missionary came to see how she was doing, she was dismayed to find the African pulling each garment through the wringer with all her might. She was dripping with perspiration and still had more loads to wash. She had forgotten about the need to turn the lever that would provide power to the rollers.

Are you pulling your struggles through the wringer of life with powerless self-effort? Remember God never promises relief from difficulties but He does promise us the strength to handle them. That strength is in the limitless power of the Holy Spirit of God. All we have to do is get access to that power. How do we do that?

ACKNOWLEDGE HIM

We have probably all experienced the rejection of a preschooler who insists on tying his own shoelaces. We stand there, our fingers itching to help his fumbling little fingers. We could accomplish it in half the time he takes to do the job. Aren't we a lot like that preschooler? The Holy Spirit is standing by ready to help us. But either we stubbornly refuse or don't even acknowledge His presence and ability to help us.

Perhaps it's a lack of understanding that causes the disregard. We seem to know more about God the Father and the Lord Jesus Christ than we do about the Holy Spirit. Let's change that, shall we? By becoming better informed, we will be better able to understand and respect the third wonderful person of the Godhead, the Holy Spirit. For the key to Christian life is trusting the Holy Spirit within us rather than the power of our own spirit. The power of the Holy Spirit of God is our source of strength to overcome self and our sinful nature. It is vitally important that we understand and acknowledge Him.

First, we need to acknowledge that the Holy Spirit is the third person of the Trinity: God the Father, God the Son, and God the Holy Spirit. He is a person—not in physical form but in spirit—and He has a personality.

THE PERSONALITY OF THE HOLY SPIRIT

As a person who has a close relationship with us, the Holy Spirit has many responsibilities. He teaches, intercedes, regenerates, and fills us. He reproves and corrects us and leads us in our daily walk.

The Holy Spirit also has feelings. He can be hurt and grieved when we are disobedient; He rejoices in our victories. When we are in close fellowship with the Holy Spirit, we experience His power, guidance, and instruction, and we gain a sense of completeness in His sufficiency to meet our every need.

THE BAPTISM, INDWELLING, AND SEALING

The baptism of the Spirit is the act of the Holy Spirit placing the new child of God into the Body of Christ. 1 Corinthians 12:13 says we are all baptized by one Spirit into one body, regardless of our nationality or station in life. We are joined into a living and lasting union with all other believers. According to Romans 6:1–4, when the Holy Spirit baptizes us into the Body of Christ, we become identified with Christ in His death, resurrection, and glorification.

The Scriptures never exhort us to be baptized by the Spirit because this transpires automatically the moment we accept Christ as our Savior. But as we will see later, Scripture does exhort us to be filled with the Spirit (Ephesians 5:18).

We are not to confuse the indwelling and sealing of the Holy Spirit with the filling of the Holy Spirit. The indwelling is a sanctifying of new believers, setting them apart for God. Chafer and Walvoord state,

> The indwelling of the Holy Spirit is represented as God's seal in three passages in the New Testament (2 Corinthians 1:22; Ephesians 1:13; 4:30). In every important respect, the sealing of the Spirit is entirely a work of God. Christians are never exhorted to seek the sealing of the Spirit, as every Christian has already been sealed. The sealing of the Holy Spirit, therefore, is just as universal as the indwelling of the Holy Spirit and occurs at the time of salvation. . . . Even if they (Christians) sin and grieve the Spirit, they nevertheless are sealed unto the day of redemption, that is, the day of resurrection or translation, when they would receive new bodies and would no longer sin.[1]

These are facts to be accepted by faith, not experiences to be sought after. The Holy Spirit's seal guarantees our permanent position in the family of God.

How precious and important these truths are to believers. With such security comes unlimited freedom to be all God wants us to be. It also places a great responsibility on the Christian not to exploit God's grace by continuing to live to self. It reminds me of Paul's question, "What shall we say, then? Shall we go on sinning so that grace may increase?" Then we can hear Paul pounding the pulpit as he shouts, "By no means! We died to sin; how can we live in it any longer?" (Romans 6:1–2). Okay, Paul, what's next?

THE FILLING

I am persuaded that we are coming to the crux of the problem of why Christians live defeated lives. It seems that Christians see the indwelling and the filling of the Holy Spirit as one and the same. But it isn't. Then what does it mean to be filled?

Here is one definition: "It's a spiritual state where the Holy Spirit is fulfilling all that he came to do in the heart and life of the individual believer. It is not a matter of acquiring more of the Spirit, but rather of the

Spirit of God acquiring all of the individual'' (italics mine).[2] To be filled means to be controlled and empowered by the Holy Spirit.

The filling is a repeated process. It is related to Christian experience, power, and service. It is our responsibility to continue being filled. Our spiritual maturity is based on our obedience to being filled.

Pentecost was the dawning of a new age. The filling of the Spirit was seen in only a few select people up to that time, but with Pentecost, the Holy Spirit would fill every person who became a child of God.

To be filled is a command. Ephesians 5:18 says we are to be filled with the Spirit. Literally translated it means "keep on being filled." If we do not keep on being filled, we are disobeying God's command. It is failure on our part not to permit God's Spirit to fill our lives. Even though we are indwelt and sealed, we may not always be filled.

All children of God may be filled by the Spirit if they meet the conditions. Ah, you knew there was a catch, didn't you. But the conditions are possible and can make a dull relationship with God fresh and exciting.

WHAT ARE THE CONDITIONS?

There are three conditions for being filled with the Spirit.
1. Not quenching the Spirit (1 Thessalonians 5:19)
2. Not grieving the Spirit (Ephesians 4:30)
3. Walking in the Spirit (Galatians 5:16)

1. Quenching the Spirit

To quench the Spirit is to stifle or suppress Him. It's our old nature rising to claim authority saying, "My will" instead of imitating Christ by saying, "Not my will, but yours, be done" (Luke 22:42).

The opposite of quenching the Spirit is yielding to the Word of God, yielding to the principles of God's Word, and yielding to God's providential acts in our lives.

The Essence of God

Philippians 2:5−11 gives us a good example of being yielded. It begins telling us our attitude should be the same as that of Christ Jesus. What was His attitude? Obedience in yielding to God the Father. God chose where He was to go—earth; how—in human form as a man; and what He was to do—give His life. God had a plan and Christ fulfilled that plan. We need to have the same sincere attitude of yieldedness if we want to be filled with the Holy Spirit.

2. Grieving the Spirit

"And do not grieve the Holy Spirit" literally translated means to stop grieving Him. That the Holy Spirit is grieved indicates sin is already present in the believer's life. This condition hinders His work, and the believer becomes powerless, making the indulgence of sin all the easier.

The remedy to grieving the Holy Spirit is to confess our sins. He has promised to cleanse us if we confess or have a change of attitude (1 John 1:9). Confession of sin establishes a new intimacy with God Himself, and fellowship is restored.

A word of warning is needed here. It is a serious thing to continue grieving the Holy Spirit. If a Christian does not stop grieving the Spirit, then God will step in with His divine discipline (1 Corinthians 11:31−32). Remember, we sin because we want to not because we have to. To continue in sin is to become a slave to sin. A true child of God does not have to be a slave to sin.

The heart is deceitful, and the tongue is untamable. The two will produce unwholesome talk if we are not relying on the strength of the Holy Spirit daily to keep a guard on our thoughts before we speak. His desire is for us to communicate encouragement, truth, love, and wisdom through wholesome conversation. We are to build one another up and that is done through the medium of the mouth in conversation with others and with God in prayer.

Mirror Mirror

The power of the Holy Spirit of God is our source of strength to overcome self and the sin nature. Let's lay hold of that power and stop grieving the Holy Spirit.

3. Walking in the Spirit.

Are you plagued by the desires of a sinful nature? Galatians 5:16 says, "So I say, live by the Spirit, and you will not gratify the desires of the sinful nature."

Chafer and Walvoord remind us,

> Walking by the Spirit is an act of faith. It is depending upon the Spirit to do what only the Spirit can do. The high standards of the present age—where we are commanded to love as Christ loves (John 13:34; 15:12) and where every thought is commanded to be brought into obedience to Christ (2 Corinthians 10:5)—are impossible apart from the power of the Spirit.[3]

Every Sunday School class I've attended has discussed the seemingly impossible and illogical concept of praying without ceasing, giving thanks for everything, and rejoicing even when you are hurting. How can a Christian have victory over the flesh and the devil, be always in a state of prayer, give thanks for everything, and rejoice evermore? It is only possible through complete dependence on the Holy Spirit of God. Are you an independent adult, ready to become God's dependent child?

There's a phrase that is glibly repeated over and over today to the total frustration of many believers. It is "Let go and let God." Now that we have studied the filling of the Holy Spirit, that phrase has more strength, doesn't it? Letting go of anything that replaces your dependence on God is not a passive act. Rather it is an active display of faith. We are always responsible for being obedient by walking resolutely with Christ, not sitting back and vegetating. It is by faith that we gain the enabling power of God through the Holy Spirit to achieve all that he has planned for us. What a beautiful partnership! Let the Spirit of God have control of the direction of your life today.

Why don't you put the book down for a moment now and express your faith through prayer to God, confessing that self has been in control and you want the Holy Spirit to fill your life anew. As you confess your sins, rely on the Holy Spirit to bring to mind those you've ignored or forgotten. Seek the cleansing of Christ's blood for each one. Then thank Him for restoring you to full fellowship. Now in faith trust the Holy Spirit to guide you, convict you, and help you not to harbor sin in your life. Do not grieve Him.

ABUNDANT FRUIT

If you are committed to keeping filled with the Spirit, you will notice that God's Word will have a greater importance to you. Reading and studying it will enrich your life. You will want to share it with others.

The Holy Spirit will now be able to guide you and teach you in spiritual truth as you read God's Word. It is only Spirit-filled people who are taught the deep things of God when the Holy Spirit reveals the Word of God to them.

Your prayer life will be revitalized. True praise and thanksgiving will become a delightful reality when you realize you are not the only one praying on your behalf. The two best prayer warriors anyone can have are praying for you as well—the Holy Spirit and Christ Jesus. Walking in the Spirit assures you of an effective prayer life (Romans 8:26).

The Holy Spirit will guide you and give you assurance of your salvation. He will enable you to worship truly and love God. True praise and thanksgiving are impossible without the assistance of the Holy Spirit. Peace and joy will also be evident in your serving the Lord and in exercising both your natural and spiritual gifts.

Finally, others will recognize you as God's child by the fruit of the Spirit evident in your life. Chafer and Walvoord express this beautifully.

> A Christian walking in the power of the Spirit experiences a progressive sanctification, a holiness of life in which the fruits of the Spirit (Galatians 5:22–23) are fulfilled. This is the supreme manifestation of the power of the Spirit and is the earthly preparation for the time when the believer in heaven will be completely in the image of Christ.[4]

With the enabling power of the Holy Spirit, you will begin to experience the godly fruit of love, joy, peace, patience, kindness, goodness, faithfulness, gentleness, and self-control. Rehearse those beautiful character traits again. Are they evident in your life? Peter Gillquist says in his book *Let's Quit Fighting About the Holy Spirit,* "The fruit of the Spirit . . . takes precedence even over the gifts of the Spirit. Christian character is always before Christian ministry."[5] The end result of a Christlike character is ministry—serving the Lord.

REVIVAL IS WHAT WE NEED

We hear much about the need for revival today. Certainly we all would agree there is a need. But what is revival? Revival is not evangelistic meetings in the church to reach the unsaved. Revival is God's children responding to the convicting power of the Holy Spirit, believers seeking the filling of the Holy Spirit of God in their lives. It's lives renewed from within and shining without. Revival is the church's displaying a lifestyle of heavenly activities.

Have you been praying for a revival? Then let the revival start in your life by allowing the Holy Spirit of God to glorify Christ in and through you, by living righteously and not grieving the Holy Spirit of God, by letting the essence of God shine through the design He created just for you.

The Essence of God

* * *

May the grace of the Lord Jesus Christ, and the love of God, and the fellowship of the Holy Spirit be with you all.

2 Corinthians 13:14

* * *

YOUR SPIRITUAL WORKOUT

1. Write your own definitions of "to grieve" and "to bring glory." Take a moment to review your life. Jot down which areas of your life are grieving the Holy Spirit. Now jot down the areas that are bringing glory to Christ.

2. Relate a time when you asserted your self-will instead of submitting to the Holy Spirit. What were the results? How did you feel about it?

3. Select one of the three conditions for being filled with the Holy Spirit and write a summary paragraph.

4. What are some of the benefits when you have a willing spirit of dependency on the Holy Spirit rather than a self-sufficient spirit of an independent adult?

5. Are you ready to commit yourself to wholesome talk with the enabling power of the Holy Spirit? Make a list of the ways you will assist yourself in perseverance. One way might be to ask your spouse or best friend to admonish you lovingly when you slip.

6. Ask a Christian friend if he understands the meaning of revival. Be ready to share what you have learned.

NOTES

[1] Lewis Sperry Chafer and John F. Walvoord, *Major Bible Themes,* rev. ed. (Grand Rapids: Zondervan, 1975).

[2] Ibid.

[3] Ibid.

[4] Ibid.

[5] Peter E. Gillquist, *Let's Quit Fighting About the Holy Spirit* (Grand Rapids: Zondervan, 1974).

Blemishes

A Hollywood photographer said recently that Elizabeth Taylor has the most beautiful complexion of any woman he has ever photographed.

Beautiful complexions are so lovely to look at. Just think—no acne, warts, freckles, birth marks, age spots, or scars to leave us with a less than healthy surface image.

Almost all of us suffer from some type of skin blemish, and so the cosmetic industry strives to meet the need of every woman's problem. They keep us looking almost wrinkle free and healthy even if we aren't.

Women's magazines regularly devote space to the art of applying make-up and taking care of the skin. One cosmetologist was asked by *McCall's* magazine how to maintain a youthful skin. She replied,

> Youthful skin? It's easy. Don't drink, don't smoke, don't get too much sun, don't use soap on your skin after the age of thirty, don't exercise your face, don't make a lot of facial expressions, do wear dark glasses in the sun, do get eight hours of sleep, do try to be happy, and do have a good lover. You'll look younger, I promise.[1]

She left out the most important requirement: being totally committed to an obedient, loving relationship with Christ Jesus. Sin ages us faster than the sun can.

BLEMISHES ARE MORE THAN SKIN-DEEP

We don't have a choice about the looks we inherit at birth but we certainly have a great deal of choice about how we will look in our mature years. All of us desire to be beautiful, and God desires it too. But His process is quite the reverse of the cosmetologist's. While the cosmetologist works at covering up blemishes on the skin, God works at exposing the blemishes in the heart . . . not only exposing but correcting.

When we allow Him to perform His work of art on our hearts, our faces will become His masterpieces, the serene beauty of His workmanship. Oh, we'll still have the same faces with the same blemishes, but with the blemishes of the heart cleansed, both our countenances and our conversation are renewed. That's just one of God's wonderful miracles. He allows our imperfections for our ultimate benefit. What may be a source of irritation to us can become a tool used by God to develop Christlike qualities in us.

God's Word assures us that "a happy heart makes the face cheerful" and "pleasant words are a honeycomb, sweet to the soul and healing to the bones" (Proverbs 15:13; 16:24).

GET RID OF ALL BITTERNESS

As serious as skin blemishes are to our positive surface image, heart blemishes can actually change facial appearances. In Ephesians 4:31, Paul warns us of five elements that constitute one ugly blemish. Those elements are rage, anger, brawling, slander, and malice. The blemish is bitterness.

Blemishes

Bitterness is the opposite of sweetness and kindness. It describes the sour, resentful spirit of people who brood over the injuries and slights they receive but stubbornly refuse to be reconciled.

God brings us into the world with soft, smooth skin, big innocent eyes, and supple little lips. We are the ones who add the worry and/or anger lines; we stiffen the jaw and distort the lips. Being filled with the Holy Spirit enables us to reflect Christ. That reflection will be a countenance of contentment even in stressful times. What does your countenance reflect? Do others see His peace and love through you?

ANATOMY OF A BITTER HEART

In dissecting bitterness, we find five elements of temper revealed. Any one or all may be present depending on the depth of the bitterness. Let's review them.

1. *Rage* flows from bitterness in an outburst of uncontrolled passion and frustration.

2. *Anger* is associated with rage. It signifies an unjustifiable human emotion that manifests itself in noisy assertiveness such as shouting and abuse.

3. *Brawling* is a noisy, angry quarrel.

4. *Slander* is dishonoring, disgracing, or defaming others. It's judging people critically with intent to murder their character or reputation by spreading false statements. Slander includes cursing, abusive language, and gossip.

5. *Malice* is active ill will with a desire to harm others or do mischief. The Greek word for malice may be defined as a vicious disposition or spite.

Paul says, "Get rid of *all* bitterness, rage and anger, brawling and slander, along with every form of malice" (Ephesians 4:31, italics mine).

All five elements of bitterness bring forth verbal accusations to an offender. Often bitterness is the result of emotional abuse we have suffered from someone else. Being hurt, we retaliate in anger.

CAUSES OF BITTERNESS

Some people have harbored a bitter spirit since they were small children. Perhaps they have never consciously known a day in their lives when they haven't experienced the gnaw of bitterness in their inner being. Unfortunately, they become like the people to whom they're bitter.

Let's look at the five causes of bitterness. *First,* there is personal guilt. Romans 2:1 says, "You, therefore, have no excuse, you who pass judgment on someone else, for at whatever point you judge the other, you are condemning yourself, because you who pass judgment do the same things."

I've proven this verse to be true too many times. Over the years, we have had troubled teenagers live in our home. One girl had the habit of letting her sweaters soak for up to an hour before washing them out. It never failed; when her sweaters were soaking, someone needed the sink. Finally I impatiently told her she had to wash them out immediately.

That very same week when she came home from school and wanted to use the sink, she found *my* sweaters soaking. Now, I never soak my sweaters, but a phone call had distracted me, and then I had forgotten about them.

Interesting, isn't it, how God works? Had I talked to her kindly about it, I don't believe I would have been caught up in the same act later. I had a resentful attitude that had been allowed to fester into bitterness, and God, in His love for me, wanted me to learn a lesson. I did learn, but when I forget, He reminds me because every time I decide to pass judgment, I find myself doing or saying the very same thing within a few days.

Second, there is the desire for revenge. Romans 12:19 says, "Do not take revenge, my friends, but leave room for God's wrath, for it is written: 'It is mine to avenge; I will repay,' says the Lord."

Why is it we are so sure we can avenge an offender better than God, who created him? It's because we want immediate revenge and find it hard to let God avenge because we don't think He ever will. By the time He gets to it, we may not be around to enjoy seeing it happen. Ah, did that touch a nerve?

If we are obedient to God's will, we will forgive, serve, and love the offenders. We will go on as though they never offended us. An interesting thing happens if we are obedient to God. We will grieve and sorrow when God does avenge them. If we can truly forgive, we will show more concern for the offenders than we did before.

Third, we get caught up in temporal values. In Luke 12:13–15 Jesus warns us to watch out and be on our guard against all kinds of greed, for a man's life does not consist of many possessions. Here He answers a man's question about dividing an inheritance. We become too concerned about getting our fair share, but God's ways would be to give to those in need. Bitterness creeps in when our expectations, demands, and what we see as our rights are not met.

Fourth, we nourish bitterness when we take up another person's offense. God allows certain trials in each of our lives to stretch us and conform us to the image of his dear son, Jesus Christ. When those occasions are upon us, He gives us the extra grace we need to cope with them. We may be offended for a time but we will get over it, and because of God's grace, we will be able to see it in proper perspective.

The important thing to keep in mind is not to share your grievance with anyone but the one who did the offending. Why? Because those on the sidelines do not have God's grace for your problem. When you are able to talk with the offender without accusing him, you need to calmly work together toward a resolution. Even if you agree to disagree, fellowship can still be restored and bitterness dissolved.

As a young boy, one of my sons had a falling-out with a good friend. Over lunch he told me his grievance, and I listened sympathetically. I picked up his grievance, made it my own, and called his friend. Without giving the boy a chance to share his side of the story, I scolded him. It wasn't until later I found out my son had been wrong. I was grieved over my thoughtless action. After praying about it, I called the boy and apologized. He graciously accepted my apology and acted as though nothing had ever happened. I knew he had truly forgiven me.

What I didn't expect was that the boy's mother had taken up his offense at me. While her son had God's grace to forgive me, she didn't. She was greatly injured over my accusations to her son. When I went to her seeking her forgiveness, she was unable to forgive me. I will always appreciate her ability to be honest with me at that moment. I knew where I stood with her—there were no false pretenses. It enabled me to pray with true understanding, and her honesty made me love her all the more.

Almost a month went by. One Sunday morning after the worship service, she came up to me, put her arms around me, and through tears told me she had forgiven me. What a beautiful moment that was. I knew the joy of genuine forgiveness from a friend. But none of that would have been necessary if I had not taken up my son's offense in the first place.

Giovanni Guardeschi wrote in *My Home, Sweet Home,* "The man who offers an insult writes it in sand, but for the man who receives it, it's chiseled in bronze."[2] Proverbs 15:4 says, "The tongue that brings healing is a tree of life, but a deceitful tongue crushes the spirit." The tongue can crush or can heal. We make the choice every time we open our mouths.

Fifth, an ungrateful attitude produces bitterness. An ungrateful attitude appears when people focus on their rights instead of on their responsibilities. No matter what others try to do for such people, it's never good enough. Perfectionists usually fit this category. They can never be pleased with others or themselves. The only way they can be perfect is by comparing themselves with others, which requires reducing others down to size. In this way,

> Perfectionists lose sight of quality of life in their measurement of quantity. Order takes precedence over relationships. Their expectations are more important than acceptance and love. They can only see perfect and imperfect, so they are unable to enjoy any activity or person that would leave them in between.[3]

BITTER CONSEQUENCES

Harboring bitterness has consequences . . . some of them devastating. I notice that the consequences don't usually appear immediately. Bitterness brews a long time. Doctors say a bitter spirit causes a change in the body's chemical balance. When we harbor bitterness, we're not able to eliminate it because it becomes absorbed into our systems. A bitter spirit immediately affects the actual marrow of the bones.

Dentists find that many patients complaining of aching teeth have only one thing wrong. They're bitter. Bitterness causes the muscles in the jaws to tighten, and the result is aching teeth. Psychiatrists also trace depression back to a bitter spirit.

Physician S. I. McMillen states in his book *None of These Diseases:*

> Running people down does not keep us free from a host of diseases of body and mind. The verbal expression of animosity toward others calls forth certain hormones from the pituitary, adrenal, thyroid, and other glands, an excess of which can cause disease in any part of the body. Many diseases can develop when we fatten our grudges by rehearsing them in the presence of others.[4]

Suppression of bitter language is not enough. We must make a conscious effort to use language that will edify others.

All this evil fruit of bitterness comes forth from the heart and spills out of the mouth. Therefore, "above all else, guard your heart, for it is the wellspring of life. Put away perversity from your mouth; keep corrupt talk far from your lips" (Proverbs 4:23–24). James 1:26 reminds us "If anyone considers himself religious and yet does not keep a tight rein on his tongue, he deceives himself and his religion is worthless."

Dr. McMillen also stated,

> In the 1930's, specialists in psychosomatic medicine began to learn that a host of *physical diseases* were caused by envy, jealousy, self-centeredness, resentment, fear and hatred—*the identical emotions that the Bible lists as attributes of our wolfish nature. Hence, we see that most of the mental and physical ills of man are caused by the activities of an inner evil force.*[5]

We have been dealing with very heavy consequences. Remember, they started from just a thought. But the thought grew into a cluster of thoughts that finally grew into a disease. In sharing a personal account of how bitterness grew in his life, David Hazard writes "I've discovered it's the small root pressing through the crack that eventually splits the rock— the small argument that escalates into a broken friendship, years of lesser 'neglects' that add up to divorce, a pile of minor disagreements that can estrange parent from child."[6] It's important that we learn to spot potential bitterness before it grows into a disease, not just to spare ourselves of unnecessary illness but more importantly, so we will honor and glorify the Lord Jesus Christ with our whole being—from the inside out.

HEALING FOR THE SOUL

As rage, anger, brawling, slander, and malice are the elements of bitterness, so joy, peace, patience, kindness, goodness, faithfulness, gentleness, and self-control are the elements of love. As bitterness is the work of the devil, so love is the work of the Holy Spirit. We must be rooted and grounded in love. Where hate once lived, love must now live.

In Philippians 2:3 Paul gives us good advice to help us keep a balanced perspective. "Do nothing out of selfish ambition or vain conceit, *but in humility consider others better than yourselves*" (italics mine).

A servant's heart is bent on restoring, building, and promoting others. It desires to see people become successful and will help them where help is needed. It is compassionate, knowing that "Compassion can bring acceptance and acceptance can give birth to love."[7] Compassion is a character trait of our Lord. He gives it to us as our badge of authority, for we are His beloved children.

Isaiah 58:9–11 shows what will happen if we do away with the yoke of oppression, the pointing finger, and malicious talk. If instead we spend ourselves on behalf of the hungry and satisfy the needs of the oppressed, only then will our light rise in the darkness and our night become like the noonday. The Lord will guide us always; He will satisfy our needs and strengthen our bodies. In the preceding verses, the Lord reveals His will for us. We are to loose the chains of injustice, free the oppressed, feed the hungry, provide shelter for the poor wanderer, clothe the naked, and provide for our own families. *Then,* He says, our healing will come quickly.

Dr. David Seamands offers good counsel in *Healing for Damaged Emotions.*

> The healing process must include the courage to unmask the anger, bring it out before God, and put it on the Cross where it belongs. There will be no healing until it is acknowledged, confronted, and resolved. Resolution means forgiving every person involved in that hurt and humiliation; it means surrendering every desire for a vindictive triumph over that person; it means allowing God's forgiving love to wash over your guilt-plagued soul."[8]

Dr. Seamands later discusses Romans 8:28, "And we know that in all things God works for the good of those who love him. . . ." He says,

> *God* works in and through the things, causing circumstances to work out for our good. . . . That God causes all things to work together for good is the greatest part of the entire healing process; that He can change hurtful insights to helpful outreach is the greatest miracle of all.
>
> Without this, the healing could not be considered total, for total healing is more than soothing painful memories, more than forgiving and being forgiven of harmful resentments, even more than the reprogramming of our minds. Healing is the miracle of God's recycling grace, where He takes it all and makes good come out of it, where He actually recycles our hang-ups into wholeness and usefulness.[9]

God can relax the rigid jaw. He can put a smile back on the lips. With His help, joy can once again sparkle in the eyes, and loving words will come from the heart to ears eager for truth and acceptance. The test of real beauty is our response to those around us. We may have failed the test in the past but we always have another opportunity to grow more beautiful for Christ by the way we mature in our relationships.

In Philippians 3:13 the apostle Paul tells us how to handle failure. "But one thing I do: Forgetting what is behind and straining toward what is ahead, I press on toward the goal. . . ." It's good advice. Don't dwell on the past but look to the task at hand and the goal before you. Christ has forgiven you, and you have a new day before you. Use it. There will be future failures, since we're not perfect yet. Just confess them and always press forward. Then Paul adds, "All of us who are mature should take such a view of things" (v. 15). Right, Paul! It's up to us. We can make our mature years even more beautiful than when we were in the fresh bloom of youth.

* * *

Blemishes

God loves us the way we are, but he loves us too much to leave us that way!

Sign on Christian Assembly Church
Seaside, Oregon

* * *

YOUR SPIRITUAL WORKOUT

1. Ask someone you're able to be vulnerable with to tell you what your countenance reveals when you're relaxed. Ask him or her to be honest.

2. Think of a particular time when you took up another person's offense. Detail the steps that occurred beginning with the moment you sympathized with the offended party to the conclusion. Is there still a need to forgive or be forgiven?

3. Memorize Philippians 2:3.

4. Alice keeps an ugly rock on her kitchen window sill near her phone. On the rock she has painted, "Alice's First Stone." Study John 8:1–11. Such a reminder has been instrumental in guiding her to limit her conversations about others to that which is edifying, encouraging, and positive. Why don't you find a stone that can act as your reminder that God accepts you unconditionally and you should do the same for others.

5. Chart your attitude for one week. Be sure to write down the times you praised and encouraged as well as the times you criticized or gossiped. Every time you write down a positive attitude, reward yourself with something you enjoy, such as a half-hour break to read, or calling a friend, or going for a walk.

6. Of the five causes of bitterness discussed, which one is most likely to entrap you? What personal steps can you take to avoid it?

NOTES

[1] "Why Some Women Age Faster Than Others," *McCall's* (November 1982).

[2] Giovanni Guardeschi, *My Home, Sweet Home* (New York: Farrar, Straus and Giroux, 1966).

[3] Jennifer James, ed., *The Slug Manual: The Rise and Fall of Criticism* (Seattle: Inner Cosmos, 1984).

[4] S. I. McMillen, *None of These Diseases* (Westwood, N.J.: Fleming H. Revell, 1963).

[5] Ibid.

[6] "Getting the Better of Bitterness," *Today's Christian Woman* (Winter 1981–82).

[7] David A. Seamands, *Healing for Damaged Emotions* (Wheaton, Ill.: Victor, 1981).

[8] Ibid.

[9] Ibid.

Seventy Times Seven

Rows of hatch marks were carefully grouped into sets of five. Their neat little columns roamed up and down and around the paper, nearly covering it from border to border. I carefully squeezed in the last few sets of marks counting softly to myself as I did so, "475, 480, 485, 490!" Finally, I was finished.

With this strangely decorated paper before me, I reread Christ's teaching about forgiveness in Matthew 18. Peter had just asked, "Lord, how many times shall I forgive my brother when he sins against me?" How like Peter impulsively answering his own question, "Up to seven times?" Surely he thought this was a generous offer. After all, the standard of the rabbis only demanded forgiveness up to three times. But Jesus turned to Peter and answered, "I tell you, not seven times, but seventy times seven."

With my hatch-marked paper serving as a visual aid, it was obvious Christ was not giving a literal number of four hundred and ninety. What folly to think we could keep track of others' offenses up to that number!

Can you imagine the record books we would have to lug around to keep score on everyone we meet? Christ gave an exaggerated figure demonstrating we are to be continuous in our forgiving without regard to the number of times we are offended.

LESSONS FROM A PARABLE

After answering Peter's question, Christ continued with a story to give us additional insights concerning forgiveness. He told of a king who was settling up the debts in his kingdom. One servant owed him a vast sum of money. It was an amount much greater than the servant could ever repay in his entire lifetime. When the servant prostrated himself before the king and begged for an extension of time, the king was moved with compassion and forgave the entire debt.

A fellow-servant owed the forgiven man an infinitesimal amount of money. He also begged for an extension of time. But the forgiven man refused to show mercy and had the debtor thrown into prison. When the king found out, he recalled the first servant and questioned him about his refusal to show compassion when he himself had been forgiven so much. The king then turned him over to the tormentors.

The parable ends with the stern warning spoken by Christ, "This is how my heavenly Father will treat each of you unless you forgive your brother from your heart."

In this parable, the king represents our merciful heavenly Father. The contrast between the enormous debt of the first servant and the trifling amount of the second paints a vivid picture. Nothing that men can do to us will ever compare with the vast wrongs we have committed against a holy God in thought, word, and deed.

In *Healing for Damaged Emotions,* Dr. David Seamands makes reference to the tormentors mentioned in this parable. As Dr. Seamands counsels with people who have harbored unforgiveness, he sees them being tormented by guilt, resentment, strife, and anxiety. He states that these produce stress, conflict, and all sorts of emotional problems—all resulting from the torments of unforgiveness.[1]

Finally, Christ's warning at the end of the parable teaches us that as we have experienced God's forgiveness, we are accountable to extend forgiveness to others. This great truth runs all through the New Testament.

Before considering some other passages, take a minute to get a piece of paper and pencil and keep them handy. As we get to the end of this chapter, each of us will have a specific list of what we need to do in extending forgiveness to others. It will be good to write the list down while it is fresh in our thoughts.

GOD HAS A BETTER WAY

Now let's think for a moment about the contrast between what Christ teaches and what the world teaches. In most cases, our society encourages us to retaliate, even the score, get restitution. God teaches us time and time again that He has a better way: forgiveness. It is an urgent message and one we must heed.

It is said familiarity breeds contempt. More likely where God's Word is concerned, familiarity breeds complacency. How often we recite the Lord's Prayer (Matt. 6:9–13) without meditating about what we are asking. As Christ teaches us to pray, He tells us the terms by which we are to ask forgiveness, "Forgive us our debts, as we also have forgiven our debtors." His teaching about prayer ends with this admonition, "But if you do not forgive men their sins, your Father will not forgive your sins" (Matt. 6:15).

Readiness to forgive others rather than to seek revenge is evidence of our new life in Christ. It shows our identification with Him. As we forgive others, we take off the rags of our old nature and put on the royal robes of our new nature in Christ Jesus.

REFLECTING THE CHARACTER OF CHRIST

Perhaps no other section of Scripture contains the very essence of this Christlike nature more clearly than that written from the Sermon on the Mount. Nestled among the treasures in this great sermon by Christ are jewels that brilliantly radiate truths concerning how we can reflect His character when we are wronged.

These truths begin in Matthew 5:38 when Christ cites the Old Testament standard of an eye for an eye and a tooth for a tooth. It is important to realize this ancient law was not referring to instructions for private individuals. This was a principle set up for social justice within the community—a guideline for a judge to mete out a sentence that would be reasonable and fair.[2]

WHEN INSULTED . . . ENDURE

Christ moves from this Old Testament basis to the higher standard required of those who follow Him. Our first responsibility is to turn the other cheek. It is imperative to examine Christ's complete statement closely. Otherwise, we can miss a very important detail. "If someone strikes you on the right cheek, turn to him the other also" (Matt. 5:39). To grasp fully what this means, find someone who is right-handed and stand facing that person. Now ask him to pretend he is going to slap you on your right cheek. Unless the person plans to stand on his head or go through some other contortion, the only way he can administer a slap of any force to your right cheek with his right hand would be backhanded. A slap with the back of a hand was a gesture to deliver an ultimate insult or to show contempt.

Christ is picturing for us what our conduct should be when we are personally insulted. We are not to retaliate or show hostility in return. Rather, we are to be humbly willing to endure further insult.

In David Augsburger's book *The Freedom of Forgiveness*, he relates that Nikita Khrushchev, ex-premier of Russia once said, "My sole difference with Christ is that when someone hits me on the right cheek, I hit him on the left so hard that his head falls off."[3] This is hardly the sole difference between the two men. But the point is clear. The world teaches revenge when insulted; Christ teaches forgiveness.

WHAT ABOUT YOUR RIGHTS?

Jesus continued His teaching to state that if someone sues you for your tunic, you should let him have your cloak also. To understand the impact of this statement, we must realize the difference between a tunic and a cloak in New Testament times. The tunic was an inner garment made of cotton or linen. Even the poorest of men would have more than one tunic. The cloak, however, was a coveted possession, and anyone was fortunate to have even one. This was a great, blanketlike garment worn as a robe by day and used as a blanket by night. Many times the cloak was a person's only protection against the cold. No judge would ever make him give it up. It was his *right* to keep his cloak because it was his resource for survival against the elements.

Do we see the point here? How many times do we seek revenge or refuse forgiveness solely because we see it as our right to do so. "After all," we rationalize, "I was wronged; the other person's actions were unjust." Do we have a right to refuse forgiveness? No! Christ's teaching is clear. We must be willing to give up even our rights.

The experience of Corrie ten Boom is a superb example of what Christ is teaching us. She had been in a concentration camp during World

War II and had been exposed to humiliating, painful, and degrading treatment. She recalls an experience in Ravensbruck when she and her sister, along with others, were forced to walk naked past the ogling eyes of the guards to the delousing showers. She remembers one guard in particular who was known for his cruelty.

Her sister died in Ravensbruck, but Corrie made it through that terrible hell and eventually was able to forgive her enemies. Following the war years, huge audiences gathered in many meetings around the world as she shared the message of forgiveness. One time, in 1947, she came to Munich to give her message. When she had finished, a balding, heavy-set man in a gray overcoat made his way forward to where she was standing. As he approached, she realized he was that same cruel guard from Ravensbruck. He acknowledged he had been a guard there, then explained he had become a Christian and knew God had forgiven him. He then stretched out his hand and asked Corrie to forgive him.

Corrie explains that this was the most difficult thing she had ever been asked to do. As she looked at him, she no longer saw the gray overcoat, but instead a blue uniform and a visored cap with its skull and crossbones. She remembered the leering, lecherous, mocking face of an SS guard. And she hesitated. Her hand froze to her side.

Surely if ever there were a time someone could stand on his rights to refuse forgiveness, it would be now. But then she remembered the teaching of Jesus. With coldness clutching her heart, she silently cried out to Jesus to help her. And then as a sheer act of her will, she thrust her hand into the outstretched hand of the guard. In that moment of obedience, she felt the healing warmth of God flood her heart. As tears welled up in her eyes, she was able to forgive him with all her heart.[4]

MORE THAN EXPECTED

Finally in the passage from Matthew 5, Christ asks us to be willing to go the second mile. The law at the time allowed a Roman soldier to compel anyone along the way to perform menial services. The person could be required, for example, to carry baggage for a mile. He could not refuse because it was his duty. Christ was teaching his followers to volunteer to do more than was expected. Not only were they to do what was required without resentment or complaint but they were to volunteer to carry the baggage a second mile. Can't you just imagine the reaction of a Roman soldier in that situation!

Again, do we understand the point? The first mile is nothing. That is what is expected of us. It is the minimum, our obligation. There is no credit or merit in this at all. It is not until we go the second mile that we are honoring Christ. How different our impact for Christ would be in our spheres of influence if we consistently practiced an attitude of the second mile.

It has been said two persons are never more than two miles apart. If each of them would do their part and go the one mile, they would meet and their differences be resolved. Too many times, however, one is not willing to do his part. But if the other will go the second mile, they can still meet and the relationship can be restored.

In each of His illustrations, Christ teaches it is not enough just to refuse retaliation. We must also forgive. Not once, not twice, not three times, not seven times, but again and again and again. Christ also teaches we are to be humble in the face of insults. We are to give up our rights when we have been wronged. We are to go the extra mile in service to our enemies. We are not only to refuse revenge and give forgiveness but we are to go to a lot of trouble to make the relationship right.

WHY?

Why does God want us to behave in these ways? Romans 12:19–21 gives the answer. God states that revenge is His and He will repay. When we take revenge in our own hands, we are demonstrating we do not trust God to do what he has promised. We are also elevating ourselves to God's position by taking on His responsibility.

This passage from Romans also commands us to do good to our enemies. It states this will be like heaping burning coals on their heads. Our motive for doing good is to be obedient to God and bring glory to Him. The result will cause our enemies to become embarrassed and sorrowful for their unjust doings. Isn't this better than continuing the pain, anger, and bitterness that develops when evil is returned for evil?

Finally, we are enlightened by this command, "Do not be overcome by evil, but overcome evil with good" (Romans 12:21). If we respond with revenge and unforgiveness, evil will overcome us and manifest itself in all sorts of problems including the toll on our health from stress, bitterness, and broken relationships. Maurice E. Wagner, Ph.D., chaplain in a mental hospital, has observed that unresolved hostility is the underlying cause of most forms of mental illness.[5]

Instead of being overcome by evil, Jesus tells us how we can overcome evil in the other half of His commandment. The formula is simple: overcome evil with good.

OUR RESPONSE

Do you have your pencil and paper ready? Remember I said we would each have a specific list of those areas where we need to extend forgiveness. As I have studied Christ's teaching on this subject, He has continued to bring circumstances and people to my mind where I need to practice these concepts. When I am obedient, God gives beauty for ashes.

Relationships are restored; hurts are healed; and the bound are set free. I am pleased as I look into God's mirror and notice that my actions are reflecting His presence.

Now are you ready for your list? Take a few moments of silent prayer before the Lord asking Him to begin a work in your heart. Now review Christ's principles concerning forgiveness. As you examine each one, ask the Lord what he would have you do.

Whatever God lays upon your heart, whomever God brings to your thoughts, wherever God directs you—write these down. This, my beloved, is your list. It is a list personally delivered to you from God. What will you do with it?

* * *

Forgiving others does not change the past—it changes the future.

* * *

YOUR SPIRITUAL WORKOUT

1. How does Christ's teaching about forgiveness conflict with the general attitude of society?

2. Meditate on Christ's words: "But if you do not forgive men their sins, your Father will not forgive your sins." Write a paragraph concerning what this means to you personally.

3. Review the three commands from Matthew 5:38ff.
   a. When wronged, do not retaliate.
   b. When wronged, give up your rights.
   c. When wronged, do more than expected for the other person. What is the hardest for you? Why?

4. Are you *readily* able to leave the matter of revenge with God? Explain.

5. Think of someone whose life you would like to impact for God. Write out several practical suggestions as to how you could put into practice the second-mile concept. Choose one of these and do it this week.

6. Examine your list from page 125 to see if it reveals any trends or new insights about yourself. Comment on how you feel about them.

NOTES

[1] David Seamands, *Healing for Damaged Emotions* (Wheaton, Ill.: Victor, 1981).

[2] This and the following principles are adapted from William Barclay, *The Gospel of Matthew*, vol. 1, The Daily Study Bible (Philadelphia: Westminster, 1975), 162–68.

[3] Nikita Khrushchev, as cited by Steward Meacham in an address given to the Intercollegiate Peace Conference, Bluffton College, Bluffton, Ohio, on March 31, 1960; quoted by David Augsburger, *The Freedom of Forgiveness, Seventy Times Seven* (Chicago: Moody, 1970).

[4] Quoted by Corrie Ten Boom, *Tramp for the Lord* (Old Tappan, N.J.: Fleming H. Revell, 1974), which reprinted it by permission from *Guideposts* (Carmel, N.Y.: 1972).

[5] Maurice E. Wagner, "The Benefits of Forgiveness," *Psychology for Living* (April 1983).

Part III

Reflections of the Heart

Be imitators of God, therefore, as dearly loved children and live a life of love, just as Christ loved us and gave himself up for us as a fragrant offering and sacrifice to God.

Ephesians 5:1–2

A Lingering Fragrance

Be imitators of God. What a command! God expects us to imitate Him. How do we do that? We do it as dearly loved children.

Adults smile at toddlers trying to imitate their parents. They struggle so hard to be like their mommy or daddy. But that is what God wants of His children. We can't be perfect in our imitation. Just as the little child shuffles in his dad's heavy shoes, so we shuffle in our endeavors to imitate God. The toddler's devotion to his father creates in him a desire to be like his father. More than anything he wants to walk like his daddy. He wants it so much, his desire is manifested in his actual attempt. Is our devotion to God so strong within us, we have a compelling desire as dearly loved children to be like him? Even though we may be shuffling along right now, how earnestly are we striving to achieve godly character? As the toddler watches his daddy, so we observe God through studying the Scriptures.

OUR POWER SOURCE

One of the modern conveniences I have grown to appreciate most is the portable hand vacuum. It cleans small messes up so quickly without my having to lug out the heavy-duty vacuum. But it's only effective for a short duration since it is not in constant contact with its power source. When it runs down, I have to reconnect it to the power source and let it recharge.

What is the Christian's power source? We recharge our lives when we spend time with God in the reading of the Bible and in prayer and meditation on His Word. If we stay away from prayer and God's Word, we are like the hand vacuum; we begin to run down. When we start the day with God in devotions, we are charged with power. As we walk through the day encountering temptations, frustrations, anxieties, and heartbreaks, we dwindle down in spiritual energy. We need to regularly plug in with our power source for renewed spiritual energy.

QUALITIES OF GODLINESS

In earlier chapters, we have dealt with putting off old attitudes and putting on new ones. We must clothe our inner selves with attitudes that reflect the qualities of godliness outwardly. In essence, imitating God inwardly will manifest itself in outer qualities as well.

Jerry Bridges explains it,

> Some Christians have a tendency to emphasize only putting off traits of the sinful nature. They are usually very morally upright, but lacking in those gracious qualities of love, joy, and compassion. . . . But there is equal danger if we focus all our attention on such qualities as love and compassion while neglecting to deal with the vices of the sinful nature. . . . We are to put off the traits of the old self and put on the traits of the new. If we desire to be godly, we must not neglect either of these biblical emphases. [1]

A Lingering Fragrance

Paul tells us in Ephesians 5:10 to find out what pleases the Lord, so let's see what new attitudes the Lord wants us to be wearing. In Ephesians 4:32 we are told to be kind, compassionate, and forgiving, and in Galatians 5:22–23 we are told to have love, joy, peace, patience, kindness, goodness, faithfulness, gentleness, and self-control.

Colossians 3:12–14 reminds us we are to clothe ourselves with compassion, kindness, humility, gentleness, and patience. We are to bear with each other and forgive whatever grievances we may have against one another, forgiving as the Lord forgave us. And over all these virtues, we are to put on love that binds them all together in perfect unity. Finally, Philippians 4:8 says we are to think on those things that are true, noble, right, pure, lovely, admirable, excellent, and praiseworthy.

It looks like the King of Glory wants to robe his dearly loved royal children in some exquisite clothes. Notice the five virtues that are repeated in these verses: kindness, compassion, forgiveness, gentleness, and patience. Are they part of your inner wardrobe?

BUT THE GREATEST IS LOVE

"Love the Lord your God with all your heart and with all your soul and with all your mind. This is the first and greatest commandment. And the second is like it: 'Love your neighbor as yourself.' All the Law and the Prophets hang on these two commandments" (Matthew 22:37–40).

First Corinthians 13 gives us an analysis of love in nine facets: patience, kindness, generosity, humility, courtesy, unselfishness, good temper, guilelessness, and sincerity.

"This is how we know what love is: Jesus Christ laid down his life for us. And we ought to lay down our lives for our brothers. If anyone has material possessions and sees his brother in need but has no pity on him, how can the love of God be in him? Dear children, let us not love with words or tongue but with actions and in truth" (1 John 3:16–18).

> Is life not full of opportunities for learning love? Every man and woman every day has a thousand of them. The world is not a playground; it is a schoolroom. Life is not a holiday, but an education. And the one eternal lesson for us all is *how better we can love.*[2]

We have been considering strong, active, rich love: the love of God. His love reaches into the dirtiest gutter as well as into the courts of kings and queens. It is a love that does not show favoritism, a love that embraces the unlovely and the lovely alike. It's love that is tough enough to endure through the thick and thin of life.

"Love is not touchy. Love is touched. . . . Love gives the benefit of the doubt. And even if doubt persists, react in love. Don't pay back evil for evil."[3] God is love. Love is of God. Without God there is not love.

GOD'S MAJOR OBJECTIVE

God's one major objective in our lives is to conform us to the image of His Son, Jesus Christ. "For those God foreknew he also predestined to be conformed to the likeness of his Son, that he might be the firstborn among many brothers" (Romans 8:29).

Why does God want us to be conformed to the image of Jesus Christ? It is through our being made holy that Christ will be exalted as the firstborn among us. Being the resurrected and glorified Lord Jesus Christ, He will become the head of a new race that is purified from all contact with sin and prepared to live eternally in His presence. It is the children of God that make up the new race.[4]

Have you ever watched a potter make a lump of clay conform to his desired image? The clay is set on the wheel and as the potter moistens it with water and spins the wheel, his hands deftly work at shaping the clay into an item that is for some distinct purpose.

A Lingering Fragrance

We are like lumps of clay when we come to God. He has a design for us and He begins shaping us in the image of Christ for the distinct purpose of bringing honor and glory to Him through being His ambassadors to a needy world.

THE IMAGE OF CHRIST

Now we come full circle to Ephesians 5:2 that says, "And live a life of love, just as Christ loved us and gave himself up for us as a fragrant offering and sacrifice to God." Live a life of love. Christ must be the center of our lives before we can practice His love. Counterfeit lovers will be incapable of imitating Christ because all that Christ is conflicts with the carnal nature.

To "live a life of love . . . as Christ." What does that mean for the child of God? Christ was obedient to the Father in coming to earth as a baby, living among men, and finally giving His life that we might have life. This is the ultimate example of love.

Not only was Christ obedient in going to the cross but He *willingly* obeyed. There is a dramatic difference between willing obedience and grudging compliance. How often I obeyed my mother in doing the dinner dishes while at the same time rebelling in my heart at having to work instead of play. But Christ's heart and mind were one with God's. There was no hidden rebellion. He willingly gave Himself up as a fragrant offering and sacrifice to God on the behalf of sinners.

God has called us to imitate Him by loving others . . . even to the point of death if necessary. Remember, no hidden rebellion. Unlike our parents, God knows the thoughts and intents of our hearts.

We will probably never be called to sacrifice our lives for someone else. But we should be ready to do so in the attitude of our hearts. Consider for a moment—how real is your love? Would you be ready to give up your life if it would mean someone else would continue to live? Or if you could lengthen or make easier the life of another, would you? Now you're not being asked to give up your life—just to assist in lengthening someone else's. Listen with your *heart* as you read the following account from a recent *Newsweek* article:

> Because they live without addresses, the homeless are unable to receive food stamps and welfare in most states, invisible in unemployment statistics and impossible to count. Estimates range anywhere from 250,000 to 2 million nationwide, tens of thousands of whom hazard the elements every night. The largest private sponsor of shelter, the Salvation Army, provides only 42,000 beds—a drop in the bucket. The largest publicly sponsored shelter system is run by New York, which now houses 6,000. That's double the capacity of two years ago and more than during the Great Depression—but insufficient in a city where officials estimate 20,000 homeless in the under-21 category alone. The chairman of the city's Board of Health says that an average of one homeless person a day is now found dead in the streets.[5]

Is our love real? Why do we expect the government or charitable organizations to take total responsibility for the needy? With so many Christians in America today, why is it there are so many destitute people? What about each individual Christian imitating Christ and reaching out on his own initiative? If we have the ability to help the poor and needy with shelter, food, clothing, work, and even our time, we had better respond. First John 3:17 questions if we see someone in need and don't feel a deep-seated emotional concern or sympathy for them, how can the love of God be in us? Then we are admonished to love with actions and truth. The true test of love is not our verbal profession of it but our willingness to help, to be involved, to willingly rub shoulders with the nitty-gritty of life's problems.

One who has devoted her life to helping the poor and needy is

Mother Teresa. She said, "When we take part in the suffering of others, we come closer to understanding Christ's suffering for us." How well do you understand Christ's suffering for you?

THE RESULTS OF GODLY LOVE

Elisabeth Elliot tells us,

> Don't let the world around you squeeze you into its own mold, but let God remold your minds from within, so that you may prove in practice that the plan of God for you is good, meets all his demands, and moves toward the goal of true maturity.
>
> Maturity starts with the willingness to give oneself. Childishness is characterized by self-centeredness. It is only the emotionally and spiritually mature who are able to lay down their lives for others, those who are "masters of themselves that they might be the servants of others."[6]

Genuine godly love has a servant's heart. Having a servant's heart will make you more concerned about benefiting others than yourself. A servant's heart will change you from selfish to selfless; it will adjust your priorities. Selfishness will yield to a humble and submissive spirit, which wholeheartedly supports the authority over you. You will be able to allow God to lead you through the input and guidance of others. You will not demand your rights.

Love makes many demands of us. Self does not understand genuine love because only the child of God can begin to understand God's love. For this reason, we must not measure our love against that of our peers. Our only true measure is against God's love. Measuring our love against God's love is the way to develop a vibrant, genuine love. Godly love does not mind soiled hands and rearranged schedules. When there is a need, love responds.

THE FRAGRANCE OF CHRIST

As Christ was a fragrant offering to God, so are those who are in Christ. When we are cleansed from sin by the blood of Christ, we lose the stench of the world and take on the fragrance of Christ.

Millions of dollars are spent on developing, advertising, and purchasing new fragrances each year. Our culture is very conscious of smelling good. And aren't we thankful! But how often do we give thought to the fragrance we are emitting heavenward? If we have the fragrance of Christ about us, the world will notice. It's a most delightful aroma to a weary world. Do you convey the aroma of Christ to God and the world?

A life cleansed of sin by Christ and lived in absolute integrity is the only way we can be a fragrant aroma. Wearing masks, being pretentious, depending on human effort, having an unforgiving spirit, lying, cheating, lacking compassion, or anything else marring our relationship with God will keep us from possessing the fragrance of Christ. As a matter of fact, sin creates a horrid stench. Christians do have an unforgettable influence on the world. Is yours a negative or positive influence? Is your aroma fragrant or foul? When you leave the office party, when you give your opinion at mealtime, or tuck your child in at night, what is your lingering fragrance? Does it reveal the fragrant beauty of Christ?

FROM SHUFFLE TO STRIDE

Let's go back to the toddler. What happens to him in sixteen years? Suddenly he's able to wear his dad's shoes without shuffling, isn't he? He grew up.

God's children are to grow, too. At first the attempt may be a mere shuffle, but God sees the desire of the heart to be like Him and it brings Him joy. He patiently works at nurturing, loving, chastising, and encouraging us. Day by day we grow; eventually our shuffle becomes a strong stride in our walk with God.

A Lingering Fragrance

We know that the character of God is our only standard for imitation and that sinning is incompatible with living a godly life. We have learned that the life of the child of God is not characterized by rebellion because we are born of God and made holy and righteous. This godliness is manifested from inside out by the fragrant aroma of Christ.

Psalm 103:8 says, "The Lord is compassionate and gracious, slow to anger, abounding in love." There's our pattern. For God's glory, let's enlarge our borders and stretch our comfort zones. Let's worry less about being accepted by physically beautiful people and love the lonely and unlovely for Christ's sake.

Do you want to show God how much you love him? You can, by imitating Him. The result will be a beautiful and fragrant friendship with God, our heavenly Father.

*   *   *

The radiant life is the shadow of God.
Plato

*   *   *

YOUR SPIRITUAL WORKOUT

1. I love the sweet fragrance of wild violets in the spring or a freshly bathed and powdered baby. What are some of your fragrance memories?

2. From Scriptures quoted in this chapter, pick out some actions and attitudes that would be a fragrant offering to the Lord.

3. How has your spiritual battery been recharged this week?

4. Review the section, "Qualities of Godliness" and list the attitudes that are actually a part of your life.

5. From the same section, decide which attitudes are most often found missing. Pick one and write out a practical goal for how you can begin developing this in your life. Be specific and set a time limit.

6. Is there someone in your family who needs your care and love? How will you begin to bridge the gap? Write it out and schedule it on your calendar to help you get started.

NOTES

[1] Jerry Bridges, *The Practice of Godliness* (Colorado Springs: Navpress, 1983).

[2] Henry Drummond and William R. Webb, *The Greatest Thing in the World* (Kansas City: Hallmark Cards, 1967).

[3] Elisabeth Elliot, *Let Me Be a Woman* (Wheaton, Ill.: Tyndale House, 1976).

[4] John F. Walvoord and Roy B. Zuck, *The Bible Knowledge Commentary: An Exposition of the Scriptures by Dallas Seminary Faculty,* New Testament ed. (Wheaton, Ill.: Victor, 1983).

[5] "Homeless in America," *Newsweek* (January 2, 1984).

[6] Elliot, *Let Me Be a Woman.*

CHAPTER **12** BY MARILYN

Love's Reflection

One day a week I go to our city's skid row district and spend time visiting and helping the street people who drop in at the Salvation Army.

Toward the end of summer, a woman I'll call Ann was in desperate need of new shoes. The toes of her shoes had separated from the soles, and she was keeping them together with rubber bands. Knowing she had no financial aid of any kind, I wanted to help her find some shoes.

As much as Ann wanted new shoes, she would not go with me to look for them, so it took longer than I had hoped to help her. By the time I gave her the shoes, the rainy season had begun, and Ann became ill with a bad cold. I was quite worried about her for I had reason to believe she was sleeping on the street. When she wasn't there the next week, I knew she must be very sick because she had never missed a day of dropping in at the Salvation Army since I had started volunteering.

When I went back the following week, Ann was there and appeared to be feeling much better. I was genuinely relieved to see her looking so well and told her so. She said, "Well, it's because of my minister."

Eager to know which minister, I said, "Oh, really! Who?"

She said, "*You!* You found me new shoes so my feet would stay warm and dry."

I was really taken aback by her comment. My first impulse was to laugh knowing what my ministers would think of such a comment. Then, I thought, no—we should all be ministers. I am not a pastor of a church but I am to imitate Christ by ministering to the needs of others.

REALLY . . . A MINISTER?

Webster's Unabridged says a minister is an attendant or servant. It goes on to define the word as a person acting for another as his agent and carrying out his orders and designs. Christ was a minister in this world, for He carried out the will of His Father and acted as His agent. Likewise, we are agents for Christ, carrying out His desires and plans.

Now look at the definition of the verb: To minister is to attend, serve, supply, or provide. We are Christ's agents serving those He died for and providing for those in need.

There are many ramifications to ministering. Much has been written about the subject, and I encourage you to make a comprehensive study of it so you can be more effective in your service for the Lord.

It takes a committed heart to be diligent about serving others in a Christlike manner. To those we love it is a natural response, but there are so many who are not loved or aren't lovable, who desperately need to see the love of God demonstrated in practical ways. Real love is best seen by what it does.

FIRST STEP TO MINISTERING

Let's look at the first of three ways we can be brighter reflectors of God's love by becoming more effective ministers for Christ. To effectively minister, we need a compassionate heart. Our Lord has displayed compassion since the time of the Creation when He gave Adam a helper because He saw it wasn't good for man to live alone. Psalm 145:8–9 tells us, "The Lord is gracious and compassionate, slow to anger and rich in love. The Lord is good to all; he has compassion on all he has made."

I'm especially touched by the phrase, ". . . he has compassion on all he has made." When Christ's compassion fills our hearts, we can accept people where they are and help them move forward. The difference between God's compassion and ours is that His is global, ours is selective. If we are going to imitate Him, we need to be global in our compassion.

The news reminds us daily of the world's lack of compassion. History has documented man's hideous acts of violence against the helpless and innocent. The only thing worse is hearts of indifference— hearts that are neither hot nor cold but tepid . . . wanting to observe without becoming involved.

What do you feel when large crowds press around you? Notice what Jesus felt the day He fed the five thousand. "When Jesus landed and saw a large crowd, he had compassion on them and healed their sick" (Matthew 14:14). Our Lord felt compassion because he saw the people as harassed and helpless, like sheep without a shepherd. His compassion didn't stop with just seeing the crowd—it took action when he healed the sick.

When evening came, the disciples wanted Jesus to send the crowds away, but He knew the people were hungry, so He fed them. His compassion compelled Him to minister. Compassion adorns the heart like garlands of flowers, and its fragrance ministers to the weary and the needy. Are you bringing joy to God's heart by imitating—reflecting—His compassion?

THE SECOND STEP TO MINISTERING

Before His death, Jesus shared these words with the disciples:

> Then the King will say to those on his right, "Come, you who are blessed by my Father; take your inheritance, the kingdom prepared for you since the creation of the world. For I was hungry and you gave me something to eat, I was thirsty and you gave me something to drink, I was a stranger and you invited me in, I needed clothes and you clothed me, I was sick and you looked after me, I was in prison and you came to visit me."
>
> Then the righteous will answer him, "Lord, when did we see you hungry and feed you, or thirsty and give you something to drink? When did we see you a stranger and invite you in, or needing clothes and clothe you? When did we see you sick or in prison and go to visit you?"
>
> The King will reply, "I tell you the truth, whatever you did for one of the least of these brothers of mine, you did for me" (Matthew 25:34–40).

Serving others is serving our Lord. Every day of the week we have the privilege of serving the Lord, for there are needy ones all around us. But a servant's heart is contrary to humanistic philosophy. Instead of asking, "How can I help you?" people are encouraged today to stand up for their rights. How opposite to God's way.

Cultivate a servant's heart by studying the life of Christ. God tells us of Jesus, "Here is my servant whom I have chosen, the one I love, in whom I delight" (Matthew 12:18). He is our most eminent example of what God wants of us. His entire ministry on earth was one of service and culminated in the most magnificent display of godly servanthood anyone can ever accomplish: His death on the Cross.

It is interesting that at the time Christ was exhibiting His greatest sacrifice, His own disciples were exhibiting acts of selfishness that would be recorded in God's Word as examples of extreme self-centeredness. It took place at the Last Supper. While they were arguing about who among them was the greatest, a bowl of water and a clean towel rested nearby.

Jesus told them they were not to be like the kings of the Gentiles who lord it over people or like others who exercise authority. "Instead, the greatest among you should be like the youngest, and the one who rules like the one who serves. For who is greater, the one who is at the table or the one who serves? Is it not the one who is at the table? But I am among you as one who serves" (Luke 22:26–27).

Christ then knelt before them, took the towel, and washed their feet. When He finished he said, "I have set you an example that you should do as I have done for you. I tell you the truth, no servant is greater than his master, nor is a messenger greater than the one who sent him. Now that you know these things, you will be blessed if you do them" (John 13:15–17).

Our Lord is saying that if He, who is King of Kings and Lord of Lords, serves others, so must you and I.

Henry Drummond, the famous Scottish evangelist of the late 1800s, wondered once, "How many prodigals are kept out of the kingdom of God by the unlovely characters of those who profess to be inside?" It's a sobering question, isn't it. We must meet the physical and emotional needs of others before we can ask them to accept our offer for spiritual help. A gospel tract is hardly the answer when the stomach aches with hunger and the body shivers with cold.

Are you aware of a need in someone's life? Does it gnaw at your heart? Take action today by ministering with a servant's heart—the heart of our Lord.

THIRD STEP TO MINISTERING

Do not let your hearts be troubled. Trust in God; trust also in me. In my Father's house are many rooms; if it were not so, I would have told you. I am going there to prepare a place for you. And if I go and prepare a place for you, I will come back and take you to be with me that you also may be where I am. You know the way to the place where I am going (John 14:1–4).

Christ spoke those words to comfort and encourage His disciples. They have encouraged saints throughout history, and I'm no exception. Since I was six years old, those words have been hidden in my heart.

Encouragement comes from a servant's heart full of compassion. God is the author of encouragement. He spoke to the prophets of the Old Testament not only to warn and admonish but also to encourage the hearts of His children. He gave us Jesus Christ to encourage us. Then God sent His Holy Spirit to comfort us when Christ returned to glory and He gave us His Holy Word to encourage and instruct us. Such loving concern He has manifested for those He created. Doesn't it make you love Him more and more? Truly, we do love Him because He first loved us!

ARE YOU AN ENCOURAGER?

We have already seen in this book what a vital role the tongue performs in our daily lives. Rather than belittling, complaining, and criticizing, the tongue can be a beautiful instrument speaking words of grace to minister encouragement. To give hope and support to a discouraged life will also bring joy to the encourager. Both parties are blessed.

Chuck Swindoll says, "I firmly believe that an individual is never more Christ-like than when full of compassion for those who are down, needy, discouraged, or forgotten. How terribly essential is our commitment to encouragement!"[1]

Words are far more effective when they are accompanied with action. Let me share some ways my friends have encouraged me while I was writing this book.

Toward the end of writing *Mirror, Mirror,* I was letting housework go to meet my deadline. A prayer partner of mine sensed my need and frustration, not only prayed for me, but took my ironing home with her on two different occasions. What a servant's heart! She ministered to me in a practical and Christlike way. It was especially meaningful to me because I know how she feels about ironing.

Another time my doorbell rang early one morning. When I opened the door, there stood Lois, a dear friend of Alice's and mine. She was holding two long-stemmed red roses with a card. She handed them to me and said, "I don't know why you need these roses, but the Lord kept telling me I had to bring them to you and Alice."

Teary-eyed, I looked at our dear friend. She was a sweet messenger of love from our Lord. Never before had I received long-stemmed red roses from the Lord. It was a special moment. I asked Lois to come in; I had to share with her why the Lord had laid such a burden on her heart.

I told her how the day before Alice and I had suffered a spirit of discouragement and that just before the roses arrived that morning, I had asked the Lord to somehow encourage us.

It was a happy visit. As Lois left she said, "I must always be alert to the Lord's nudgings because when I obey Him, I find out He's right every time."

When I went to work with Alice, I handed her God's personal gift of encouragement. That was all that was needed. God's work was sufficient, and her heart was as encouraged as mine.

Sometimes it isn't what people say or do that encourages a person as much as how they listen. Listening is also a vital part of encouragement. We need to be attentive, sensitive, and accepting of people and their feelings. We need to listen beyond the words they are sharing with us. We need to listen for what they really want to say but can't. Don't be quick to give advice. Just listen with sensitive discernment. If people have trouble expressing themselves, then help by drawing them out with questions. Give advice only when the one you're encouraging can handle it. Many times I've worked out a problem just by sharing it with a sympathetic listener. They don't have to say a word; they listen.

THE LAST STEP

Let Christ encourage you. On his radio program "Back to the Bible," Theodore Epp said, "Christ will never be able to do *through* you what he has not been allowed to do *in* you." Christ is our hope, our example, our joy. If you are not experiencing His encouragement, then spend some time with Him. Select a place of quietness, take the phone off the hook, and forget about time. Make Christ the object of your affection and let Him minister to you.

When Christ is the focus of our affection and we experience God's love, then we will share it, not with those we select but with everyone we encounter. We have a responsibility to be available, sensitive, and obedient. God's love is not a possession to hoard. He wraps you in His cloak of love for you to wrap around those shivering outside of His love. He expects us to share His love unconditionally.

God is the love; we are the mirrors. Polish your mirror with the cloth of ministry. Make it shine! Let others see Love's reflection in you. Enjoy your ministry, remembering that as we minister to others we minister to the heart of God. What a *privilege!*

* * *

But if anyone obeys his word, God's love is truly made complete in him. This is how we know we are in him: Whoever claims to live in him must walk as Jesus did.

1 John 2:5−6

* * *

Love's Reflection

YOUR SPIRITUAL WORKOUT

1. Identify three situations in the last month where you showed compassion. What motivated you to those acts?

2. Think of three situations during the last month in which you could have expressed compassion but didn't. What hindered you?

3. Identify two activities outside your comfort zone where there is opportunity to reflect God's love. How will you go about investigating them as a possible area of ministry?

4. What steps can you take to minister more effectively to a close friend?

5. Ask the Lord to make you sensitive to the needs of others around you. Is there someone to whom He would like to send a rose, a card, or a special dessert? Are you willing to be His messenger of love?

6. Do you need more encouragement? One of the best ways to be encouraged is to become an encourager. Are you willing to begin a ministry of encouragement by studying about it? If so, select the books on encouragement from our Recommended Reading List and begin studying now.

NOTES

[1] Charles R. Swindoll, *Growing Strong in the Seasons of Life* (Portland, Ore.: Multnomah, 1983).

A Love Letter

Dear Reader,

It took more than a year for us to write this book for you. A year of studying, of stretching, of experiencing our own spiritual roots, digging deeper into hard soil. It began as a labor of discipline; it ended as a labor of love.

As we reflect on the previous chapters, we are trying to put ourselves in your place and wonder how the reading will be for you. Will it be challenging? Will some sections be too hard? Too easy? Will it require perseverance? Will it be a joy? Will there be chapters that help you grow? It has been all of these for us.

More than anything, it has caused us to examine our own walks with God. At times, we seemed to be on a bright and sunny path, skipping along and seeing the way clearly before us. At other times, the way seemed obscure, and we stumbled. In our difficulty, we took comfort in knowing God was our guide and we trusted Him to show us the way. Those were the times we grew.

How is it with you, dear one? Do you struggle like us? Let us promise together to walk closer to Him in all circumstances. Let us be willing to open our hearts to God's refining process, so we may become women who reflect His righteousness and holiness.

In refining gold, the dross must be removed again and again. The task may seem long and tedious, but the results are glorious. The process is finished when the refiner can see his face reflected in the metal. So it must be with our hearts. We must not be discouraged. We have the promise of Philippians 1:6 that He who has begun a good work in us will carry it on to completion.

One day Christ will see Himself reflected in our hearts, and others will see His beauty in us. They will know such beauty flows from a heart where Jesus is Lord.

With love and praise,
Alice ♥ Marilyn

Recommended Reading

Joseph Aldrich, *Lifestyle Evangelism; Secrets to Inner Beauty*

Ronald Allen and Gordon Borror, *Worship, Rediscovering the Missing Jewel*

David Augsburger, *Caring Enough to Confront; From Here to Maturity; Caring Enough to Hear and Be Heard*

Stanley C. Baldwin, *What Makes You So Special?*

Jerry Bridges, *The Pursuit of Holiness; The Practice of Godliness*

Lawrence J. Crabb, Jr. and Dan B. Allender, *Encouragement: The Key to Caring*

Charles Colson, *Loving God*

James C. Dobson, *Love Must Be Tough; Hide or Seek*

Elisabeth Elliot, *Let Me Be a Woman*

Richard Foster, *Celebration of Discipline*

Peter Gillquist, *Let's Quit Fighting About the Holy Spirit*

Phillip Keller, *The Gardener Looks at the Fruit of the Spirit*

Tim LaHaye and Bob Phillips, *Anger is a Choice*

Karen Burton Mains, *Open Heart, Open Home*

S. I. McMillen, *None of These Diseases*

Earl D. Radmacher, *What to Expect from the Holy Spirit*

Frankie Schaeffer, *A Time for Anger: the Myth of Neutrality*

David A. Seamands, *Healing for Damaged Emotions*

Charles R. Swindoll, *Encourage Me; Dropping Your Guard; Improving Your Serve*

Norman Wakefield, *Listening: A Christian's Guide to Loving Relationships*

Philip Yancey, *Where Is God When It Hurts*